Special Education
Case Studies

Special Education Case Studies

for Ontario Classrooms

Kimberly Maich
Randy Hill

OXFORD
UNIVERSITY PRESS

OXFORD
UNIVERSITY PRESS

Oxford University Press is a department of the University of Oxford.
It furthers the University's objective of excellence in research, scholarship,
and education by publishing worldwide. Oxford is a registered trade mark of
Oxford University Press in the UK and in certain other countries.

Published in Canada by
Oxford University Press
8 Sampson Mews, Suite 204,
Don Mills, Ontario M3C 0H5 Canada

www.oupcanada.com

Library and Archives Canada Cataloguing in Publication
Maich, Kimberly, 1969-, author
Special education case studies : for Ontario classrooms
/ Kimberly Maich and Randy Hill.

Includes bibliographical references and index.
ISBN 978-0-19-902217-5 (softcover)

1. Special education—Canada—Case studies. 2. Inclusive
education—Canada—Case studies. I. Hill, Randy (Randall
Gordon), author II. Title

LC3984.M35 2017   371.90971   C2017-902565-1

Cover image: © Albert Veress/123RF
Cover and interior design: Sherill Chapman

Oxford University Press is committed to our environment.
Wherever possible, our books are printed on paper which comes from
responsible sources.

Printed and bound in Canada
2 3 4 — 22 21 20

Contents

Susan Elizabeth Hill
March 8, 1978 – December 19, 2016

This book is dedicated to the memory of Susan Elizabeth Hill, an angel here on earth, who brought love and joy to many every day. She inspired those who could help and teach special children like herself. Susan's journey and challenges led to the creation of this case study book.

Acknowledgements

Kimberly Maich

As always, the work of my heart and my hands would not be possible without the constant soul-saving sustenance (and delicious meals) from my husband of 26 years, John, and our delightfully diverse grown-up children: Robert, Grace, and Hannah. This book is dedicated to my first grandchild, Quincey Matthew, who I hope will grow up to be a book-eater.

Thank you to Amy Gordon and Christina Maria Jelinek, who persisted through the inevitably long editorial process of developing this book project, while providing a nice balance of making us "toe the line" but also encouragement and flexibility. Huge thanks also go to those skilled educators who consulted with us on the details included in our case studies, including Fiona Caldwell-King and Jennifer McMillan, and our very helpful peer reviewers. Enormous appreciation goes out to my persistent and knowledgeable co-author, Randy Hill, our wonderful research assistants/graduate students for this project, Monique Somma and Megan Henning, who provided invaluable support throughout. And, of course, to Sushi 8 in Brantford—thank you for providing me with many three-hour manuscript-writing lunches at my favourite table (C1—with the plug for my laptop). I will never spit on your windows.

Your assistance made this project possible—and far better!

Randy Hill

Working with my co-author, Kimberly, and our editor, Amy, on this massive undertaking has been a wonderful journey. Thank you both for all your support and guidance. I also thank Bonnie, my soulmate, and our children, Susan, Adam, and Josh, for their patience and support throughout this project.

We were fortunate to have two highly energetic and experienced research assistants, Monique Somma and Megan Henning, whose commitment made this experience go smoothly. Also, thanks to Marion Markarian, Mary McCully, and Darion Cassidy for their contributions in building several of the case stories. Other contributors remain anonymous, but we are also deeply thankful for their sharing.

My sincere hope is that this case study book will assist new and practising teachers in their understanding of children with exceptionalities and in the development of the strategies and supports needed for their success.

The Publisher

OUP Canada would like to thank the following reviewers for their helpful feedback:

- Gaby van der Giessen, Laurentian University,
- Ron Phillips, Nipissing University,
- Carolyn Salonen, Wilfrid Laurier University,
- Steve Sider, Wilfrid Laurier University, and
- Jacqueline Specht, University of Western Ontario,

as well as those who wished to remain anonymous.

Introduction

Educators—both new and experienced—learn from being in schools, but being in schools is not always possible. The accessible narratives that make up this book create an alternative to direct observation: a common landscape to critically discuss everyday happenings in school-based special or inclusive education when direct entry into the field is not possible (Thistlethwaite et al., 2012), or sometimes not desirable, due to issues with accessibility and/or confidentiality. Delving into these cases will assist readers in exploring critical incidents, practices, and/or processes in an in-depth (yet removed) manner. In turn, exploring these cases creates a type of remote entry into the landscape of teaching in inclusive, publicly funded schools, utilizing keywords, questions, and resources to consider, discuss, learn, respond to, and develop new skills that can be used on-site in Ontario classrooms.

The facts of these cases are based on real-life situations; however, in the interest of confidentiality and privacy, many facts, names, and descriptors have been changed. Special educators shared student experiences to assist us in developing valid case studies. Information was gathered through experiences within schools (e.g., practicum placements) and introductory instruction in inclusive or special education.

The cases in this text are written specifically for Ontario Certified Teachers in the Ontario school system, demonstrating the practices and processes of special and/or inclusive education practices. They were developed for teachers who have basic knowledge, understanding, and skills around what happens in Ontario schools when it comes to students with exceptionalities. More specifically, its audience is expected to be OCTs who are engaged in professional development beyond a basic program in teacher education—such as Additional Qualifications courses in (and related to) special education and/or inclusive education (Ontario College of Teachers, 2017).

However, its contents are useful and applicable for many others in the school system (e.g., registered early childhood educators, child and youth workers, etc.), as well, who are in the process of building upon their skills and knowledge in this field, which is, of course, highly applicable to all members of the K–12 school community. Lastly, this resource does have potential to be part of the basic program of teacher education if used as a supplementary tool paired with instruction and resources beyond a first, foundational course in the field.

For a reminder of some of the basic processes in Ontario special education, see Figures I.1 and I.2.

Approach

Let's talk about the style of this text.

The narratives in each case are written to be easy to read, to be easy to understand, and to reflect the narrative style shown in fictional readings—yet are never boring or repetitive. Narrative-style storytelling is ancient, fundamental

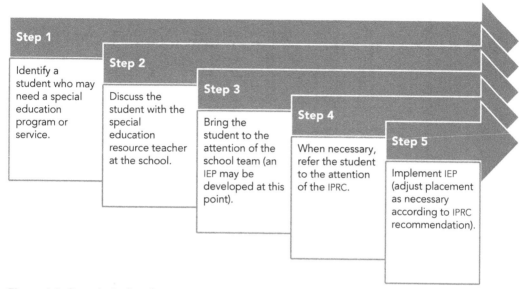

Step 1

Identify a student who may need a special education program or service.

Step 2

Discuss the student with the special education resource teacher at the school.

Step 3

Bring the student to the attention of the school team (an IEP may be developed at this point).

Step 4

When necessary, refer the student to the attention of the IPRC.

Step 5

Implement IEP (adjust placement as necessary according to IPRC recommendation).

Figure I.1 Ontario Referral Processes to Access Special Education Services
Source: Adapted from Bennett, Dworet, & Weber, 2013.

(Herreid, 1997/1998), even emotionally healing (Maich & Kean, 2004), or medicinal (Herreid, 1997/1998), utilized since the 1800s for post-secondary education (Bano, Arshad, Khan, & Safdar, 2015). Towey (2000), interestingly, emphasizes that "*fiction* works best in creating flow" [my italics] (p. 134). How convenient for the context of this book! These fictional-style narratives you are about to read will engage you and are intended to help create a feeling of flow. Please note that the use of the term "fictional-*style*" is deliberate. While the majority of these cases are simulated by the authors, one is carefully reconstructed from a historical account of real-life experience. The others reflect an aggregate of authentic, anonymous pieces of information and elements of varied professional experiences, merged together to reflect possible and probable school-based experiences.

But what is "flow"? Flow, according to its originator, Csikszentmihalyi (Csikszentmihalyi, Nakamura, & Abuhamdeh, 2014), is synonymous with the phrase "optimal experience," at the point of "dynamic balance between opportunity and ability" (p. 212), yet differentiated from either anxiety or boredom. Flow can be applied to a range of experiences (from watching television to taking Math class) and can be visualized as happening with a narrow range or channel between individual sense of challenge and level of skill (in each experience).

And what is flow within narrative-style reading? Well . . .

Flow activities require skill, an investment in mental energy, concentration and a challenge. Flow occurs when the challenge of the task and

Step One

| Every school board is required to appoint one or more IPRCs. | **Student is formally referred to an IPRC by the school's principal.** | Principal may initiate referral (notifies parent). Must initiate referral if asked by parent in writing. |

An IPRC requires a minimum of three members.
One member must be a principal or supervisory officer of the board (or designate).

Step Two

| School board must publish a detailed Parents' Guide. | **IPRC obtains and considers educational assessment. May interview student with permission of parent. Receives information put forward by school and parent. Shares all written information with parent.** | Medical and/or psychological data may be requested, subject to Health Care Consent Act (1996).

Teacher interview and/or input not required by regulation, but most school boards will include these. |

Step Three

| | **IPRC must consider all information and proposals for special education programs and services.** | Parent may present proposals in addition to those from school board. |

A parent is entitled to have a representative of choice present and may participate in all discussions except decision-making.

Step Four

| Written decision of IPRC goes to parent, referring principal, school board. Parent may request that IPRC meet again to reconsider. | **IPRC decides student is not exceptional.**

OR

IPRC identifies student as exceptional and decides on a placement. May make recommendations (but not decisions) regarding programs and services. | Process ends, unless parent appeals or requests follow-up meeting. Decision statement must list placement, category/categories and definition(s) of exceptionality, and student's strengths/needs. Placement to be regular class if it meets needs and if parent wishes. IPRC must give reasons if special class is chosen. |

Whenever parent appears, note that students 16 years and older may be part of the process, along with parent.

Step Five

| Within 30 school days principal of school where student is placed must see to development of IEP and a Transition Plan. | **Student is placed according to IPRC decision. IEP is developed and implementation begun.** | Reviews confirm existing situation or changes may be made.

Principal to review and update IEP. |

Review		
Identification and Placement How the IPRC works: A memorandum in the fall of 2006 from the then–deputy minister outlined what for some school boards across the province would be a shift in practice regarding IPRC. The memorandum suggested that school boards re-examine their procedures around IPRC and consider dispensing with a formal IPRC process in those cases where the board and parent were in agreement that that the student's placement be in the regular classroom.	**Student's situation to be reviewed at least once every school year by an IPRC. After the initial identification parents must wait three months before requesting a review to allow time for the initial identification and programming to be put in place.**	Reviews confirm existing situation or changes may be made. Principal to review and update IEP.
In cases of APPEAL: Step One		
Parent may appeal identification as exceptional, or placement, or both. Parent and/or representative entitled to participate in all discussions except decision-making.	**School board convenes a three-member Appeal Board to review the IPRC material and decisions.**	One member chosen by board, one by parent. The two select a third as chair (in case of disagreement, chair is chosen by MOE).
Step Two		
Written recommendation to parent, principal, school board, and chair of IPRC.	**Appeal Board agrees with IPRC and recommends its decisions be implemented.** OR **It disagrees with IPRC and makes recommendation to school board about identification or placement or both.**	May interview anyone Appeal Board chair feels has information to contribute. Written reasons must accompany written statement of recommendation.
Step Three		
Written decision of school board goes to all parties.	**School board considers recommendation and decides what action to take.**	School board is not limited to recommendation of Appeal Board. If parent signs consent, or if consent not signed by parent, does not appeal.
Step Four		
	School board decision is implemented.	Step Four stayed if parent appeals. Final appeal stage is to Special Education Tribunal.

Figure I.2 Identification, Placement, & Review Committee Processes
Source: Adapted from Bennett, Dworet, & Weber, 2013.

the skill of the participant are equal. Skills needed for narrative reading include concentration, literacy, an understanding of the rules of written language, the ability to transform words into images, empathy toward characters, and the ability to follow a story line. (Towey, 2000, p. 133)

However, it is important to note, "When a reader reaches a flow state while reading, it is most frequently with a text that has been self-selected. Assigned texts generally do not induce flow unless there was a previous interest in the subject by the reader" (Towey, 2000, p. 133). Therefore, this manuscript provides choice to support self-selected readings. Each major grade level is organized by chapter, and each chapter presents five cases so that the reader can choose stories of personal interest and benefit, potentially leading to a successful flow state. Yet, each case is novel—even within a grade-level division—retaining interest while attempting to balance challenge and skill in its readers. In other words, it is written with the hope that its reader might experience a "blissful state of enjoyment" (Csikszentmihalyi, Nakamura, & Abuhamdeh, 2014, p. 215) where "hours elapse in minutes" (p. 216).

But where is the learning in all of this? its reader might ask.

For the answer to this question, we move away from the experience of reading the cases, to the dissection of use of the cases themselves. Case-based teaching and learning not only delivers the opportunity to develop professional skills (e.g., contextual problem solving), but it also offers its reader the opportunity to discover and construct (or build) meaning and learning through information processing, dialogue, insight, reflection—and sense making (Bano, Arshad, Khan, & Safdar, 2015; Kantar & Massouh, 2015). In contrast to its long history of use, there is no overall consensus as to its definition. Thistlethwaite et al. (2012) suggest that case-based learning (CBL) can be defined this way: "The goal of CBL is to prepare students for clinical practice, through the use of authentic clinical cases. It links theory to practice, through the application of knowledge to the cases, using inquiry-based learning methods" (p. e422). Though the field of education is typically contrasted with clinical models, it is important to recognize that, relatively speaking, special education is likely the closest to clinical practice found in school-based experiences, and that much literature around its use is found in the context of clinical care.

Herreid (1997/1998) stipulates that cases in CBL are best when they

- tell stories,
- focus on interesting issues,
- are current,
- create empathy,
- include quotations,
- are relevant,
- have pedagogic value (in the case of this book, andragogic value),
- provoke conflict,
- force decisions,

- apply to many situations, and
- are brief.

The book you are about to embark upon meets all of these points for an exemplary CBL scenario, bar none!

Thistlethwaite et al. (2012) have developed an adapted model of CBL (see Figure I.3), which provides a visual overview, so that you can see its flow as well as envision it from what you have read so far.

In their extensive review of related research, they concluded that:

- Students enjoy CBL and think that it helps them learn better. Whether this is reflected in assessment results is far from clear; however, enjoyment can lead to increased engagement and motivation for learning, which in itself is a desirable and positive effect.
- Teachers enjoy CBL. As well as potentially making better use of teaching time available, more engaged and motivated students make for a more enjoyable teaching experience.
- CBL provides an opportunity to introduce interprofessional learning.

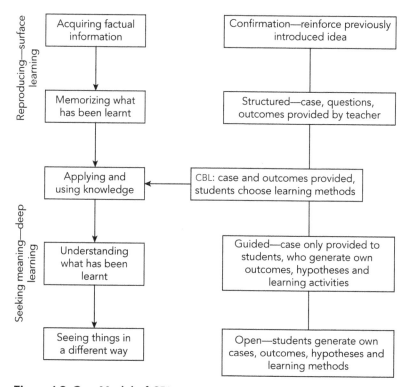

Figure I.3 One Model of CBL
Source: Adapted from Banchi & Bell, 2008, and Entwistle, 2009.

- CBL appears to foster effective learning in small groups, possibly through the effect of having more engaged learners, but perhaps also through having more structured learning activities closely linked to authentic clinical practice scenarios.
- Online CBL can work well providing attention is paid to the online learning environment. (Thistlethwaite et al., 2012, pp. e435–e436)

Educators should take these teaching points into account (e.g., group learning), keeping in mind that the questions provided are a guide to support positive outcomes (e.g., critical thinking).

Guide to Effective Use

This text is composed of this introductory chapter plus four chapters of content, focusing on primary, junior, intermediate, and senior grade levels. Each chapter, in turn, is made up of five cases. Cases are varied by point of view. For example, many cases are included from a teacher's point of view: classroom teachers, special education teachers, resource teachers, and even teacher consultants at the board level! Other cases are written from the vantage point of students, parents, and teachers, and include the voices of other members of the school community—such as friends.

All chapters follow a similar structure, including the following elements:

- A brief introduction to the chapter and its cases.
- Each case presented in narrative style.
- A list of brief response questions for each case.
- A list of in-depth response questions for each case.
- Bolded keywords for each case, defined throughout.
- Suggested resources—readings, websites, articles, and multimedia—for each case.
- A comprehensive list of chapter references.
- Varied resources, figures, and/or templates are integrated throughout the cases as well as related teaching and learning resources, as needed.

Each case has a central story, and each story has at least one central issue that plays out throughout the case in an extended manner. These issues are sometimes of critical importance—such as advocacy—but sometimes appear more peripheral to student success—such as setting up the classroom environment for specific needs. It would be a mistake, however, to judge these latter, proactive/preventative steps as *less* important than responding to emergent concerns related to inclusive education.

It is important to recognize that all cases do not represent the evidence-based practices, best practices, or even preferred practices of educators, classrooms, and schools. In fact, you might read about practices that you disagree with—or to which you object. These are some of the motivators that lead to the deep, rich discussions that lead to change, growth, and learning. The resources that support each case—especially the related questions—help learners to apply the specific processes and practices of Ontario-based special education, but also to think critically about the relationships and responsibilities of professional educators. For example, readers may not only want to discuss *what was done* but also how this could be *done differently.*

Along with these deep learnings are many opportunities for learning the foundations of Ontario's expectations around supporting students with exceptionalities, such as identification, placement, accommodations, modifications, alternative courses, Individual Education Plans (IEPs), legislation, teaching practices, and much more. Readers will *view* examples of, for instance, components of IEPs (such as assessment histories), but also develop these (such as by creating lists of accommodations and Special Education Program pages).

Readings of case stories can be accomplished with ease individually, as a group, as a class, or even with the use of technology (e.g., audio recordings, podcasts, animations). According to the literature around CBL (as noted above), cases are best discussed with others. This can be accomplished in face-to-face classes, as well as within either synchronous or asynchronous online learning environments. Those instructing such courses should pay careful attention to the included *Guide to Case Study Choice* to match case options with learning objectives, which provides a brief overview of the related exceptionalities, other considerations, key figures, main interventions and approaches, and assistive technology highlights. As choice and options are important in CBL (again, as noted above), providing multiple options for any learning objectives is recommended.

The pedagogical tools included (as noted above) can be used in multiple ways for instruction, understanding, and varied levels of diagnostic, formative, and summative assessment. For example:

- Cases could be discussed both before and after reviewing salient related literature provided in the *suggested resources*. Instructors can examine what changes have occurred in knowledge, skills, and attitudes.
- Groups of learners reading and discussing any given case could choose, develop, and share replies to the *brief response questions* provided.
- Groups of learners (or individuals) could develop lengthy responses to provided *in-depth response question(s)* as part of a project, paper, or exam.
- Learners could redefine *keywords*, apply them to their own classroom situations, and rationalize their choices as part of an online discussion.
- Learners could visit suggested websites, and rate and/or critique these sites in accordance with their perceived use in school communities.
- Learners could be asked to respond to any *brief response questions* or *in-depth response questions* and to integrate one or more *suggested resources*.
- Learners could be asked to suggest alternative interventions and/or approaches to a case, such as different choices in assistive technology.
- Learners could use the case material for the school team simulation and IEP development.

This list could continue, but instructors will of course have individual plans and preferences as to how they would best use these cases and their accompanying resources depending on their environments, courses, and the attributes of their learners at any given time. Creativity is key to any successful teaching and learning environment!

Guide to Case Study Choice

Chapter & Case Study	Grade Level	Exceptionalities (Identification or Diagnosis)	Other Considerations	Key Figures	Main Interventions & Approaches	Assistive Technology Highlights	Page #
CHAPTER 1							
Case Study 1	Grade 2	ASD	Indigenous Single-parent home Transitions	OSR Statement of Decision Assessment	Inclusive classroom Resources for teachers Suggestions for the year	n/a	2
Case Study 2	Grade 3	Multiple (LD/Autism)	Point of view of teacher (LTO) IEP meeting	Story Strengths & needs IEP team Assessment	First-year teacher Strengths-based Success-focused Problem solving	Co-Writer SEA funding	9
Case Study 3	Multi-grade (Primary)	Multiple (Intellectual/Physical)	Importance of language IEP writing	Individualized equipment list Individualized equipment Assessment	Self-contained (segregated) classroom Reverse inclusion Preparing for the school year Transition	SEA funding	13
Case Study 4	Grade 4	Gifted Query	School transitions (moving) Policies and practices around giftedness	CCAT score summary Board policy (giftedness)	Professional collaboration Assessment for identification	n/a	17
Case Study 5	Year 1 Kinder-garten	Query Physical: Blind & Low Vision	Two moms Problem behaviours	Teaching recommenda-tions IPP excerpt Note from pediatrician	Parent collaboration In-school team Transition to school	Audio books Tactile schedule	21

Chapter & Case Study	Grade Level	Exceptionalities (Identification or Diagnosis)	Other Considerations	Key Figures	Main Interventions & Approaches	Assistive Technology Highlights	Page #
CHAPTER 2							
Case Study 1	Grade 4	Multiple (ASD, MID)	Resource team meeting Developmental Coordination Disorder	Registration form Principal's notes In-school team recommendations Excerpt from psycho-educational assessment IPRC Statement of Decision Elements of a SMART IEP	Complex family situation Transition to a new school Parent collaboration and problem solving	n/a	32
Case Study 2	Grade 5	Neurodevelopmental Disorder associated with Prenatal Alcohol Exposure	New diagnosis IEP team Inclusive school leadership	Strengths, needs, and accommodations Alternative course (social skills) In-school team recommendations Power Card	Parent collaboration Interdisciplinary collaboration Alternative course Character education		39
Case Study 3	Grade 6	ASD	Multi-disciplinary support (e.g., OT)	MAS analysis Assessment list OT recommendations Team meeting notes	Educational assistant Behaviour assessment In-school team Peer buddies SLP & OT therapy Scribing	Dragon Naturally-Speaking	45
Case Study 4	Grade 4	Down Syndrome	Bullying Siblings Sign language	Restorative justice typology Modified program template Program list Alternative programs	Restorative justice	n/a	50
Case Study 5	Grade 6/7	n/a	Universal design	Calm Down Kit The relaxation station	Cozy corner Five-point scale Break card Zones of regulation Stress ball Hush bottle	Noise-cancelling headphones	56

continued

Chapter & Case Study	Grade Level	Exceptionalities (Identification or Diagnosis)	Other Considerations	Key Figures	Main Interventions & Approaches	Assistive Technology Highlights	Page #
CHAPTER 3							
Case Study 1	Grade 7	n/a	Health-related needs (e.g., severe allergies)	Student profile Knee scooter	Profiles	n/a	64
Case Study 2	Grade 8	ASD	Service dogs	Certified service dogs for autism Service dogs and children with ASD Sample letter Accommodations Safety plan	Service dog	n/a	68
Case Study 3	Grade 8	Traumatic Brain Injury	Traumatic brain injury Health-related needs (e.g., chronic pain) ASL	Environmental accommodations Transition plan	Technology Assistive technology Tutoring	FM system iPad apps Smart board Closed captioning	76
Case Study 4	Grade 8	Communication: LD	AD/HD Kinesthetic strengths	Strengths and needs Parent/student consultation IEP	Assistive technology Computer technology Video modelling Flipped classroom	Word	81
Case Study 5	Grade 8	Communication: LD	Intensive assistive tech training	Invitation to Tech Week Assessment list In-school team recommendation To-do list Placement options IEP	Response to Intervention Assistive technology	Kurzweil WordQ	90

Chapter & Case Study	Grade Level	Exceptionalities (Identification or Diagnosis)	Other Considerations	Key Figures	Main Interventions & Approaches	Assistive Technology Highlights	Page #
CHAPTER 4							
Case Study 1	Grade 11	Fetal Alcohol Effects	OSSLT Bilingual Fetal Alcohol Effects Mental health issues Legal issues	In-school team recommendations Assessment information Modified program	Applied courses Multi-disciplinary supports (e.g., guidance counsellor)	n/a	100
Case Study 2	Grade 11	Intellectual: Developmental Disability	Foster care/ Children's Aid Community-based supports	Summary Transcript Medical information Assessment information	Placement change Alternative course Safety plan Peer supports Multi-disciplinary supports (e.g., child-youth worker)	n/a	105
Case Study 3	Grade 10	Communication: Learning Disability	English Language Learner Self-advocacy Parental conflict	Note from the principal Accommodations Parent/student consultation log	Accommodations Assistive technology	WordQ + SpeakQ OSAPAC	110
Case Study 4	Grade 12	Intellectual: Giftedness	Blog style Gender identity	Assessment information Summary Goals	Leadership opportunities Private school	n/a	115
Case Study 5	Grade 1 to 12 and beyond	Communication: LD	Reflection Lifespan approach Advocacy Accommodations versus modifications	Summary Assessment report IEP	Specialized classroom Learning strategies Assistive technology	General	120

References

Banchi, H. & Bell, R. (2008). The Many Levels of Inquiry. *Science and Children, 46*(2), 26–9.

Bano, N., Arshad, F., Khan, S., & Safdar, C. (2015). Case based learning and traditional teaching strategies: Where lies the future? *Pakistan Armed Forces Medical Journal, 1,* 118–24.

Bennett, S., Dworet, D., & Weber, K. (2013). *Special education in Ontario schools* (7th ed.). St. David's, ON: Highland Press.

Csikszentmihalyi, M., Nakamura, J., & Abuhamdeh, S. (2014). Flow. In *Flow and the foundations of positive psychology: The collected works of Mihaly Csikszentmihalyi* (pp. 227–38). Netherlands: Springer.

Entwistle, N. (2009). *Teaching for Understanding at University: Deep Approaches and Distinctive Ways of Thinking.* Basilstoke: Palgrave Macmillan.

Herreid, C. (1997/1998). What makes a good case? *Journal of College Science Teaching, 27*(3), 163–5.

Kantar, L., & Massouh, A. (2015). Case-based learning: What traditional curricula fail to teach. *Nurse Education Today, 35*(8), E8–14.

Maich K., & Kean, S. (2004). Read two books and write me in the morning! Bibliotherapy for social emotional intervention in the inclusive classroom. *Teaching Exceptional Children Plus, 1*(2). http://files.eric.ed.gov/fulltext/EJ966510.pdf

Ontario College of Teachers. (2017). *Additional qualification courses and programs.* http://www.oct.ca/members/additional-qualifications/aq-courses-and-programs

Thistlethwaite, J., Davies, D., Ekeocha, S., Kidd, J., MacDougall, C., Matthews, P., . . . Clay, D. (2012). The effectiveness of case-based learning in health professional education. A BEME systematic review: BEME guide no. 23. *Medical Teacher, 34*(6), e421–4.

Towey, C. (2000). Flow. *The Acquisitions Librarian, 13*(25), 131–40. doi: 10.1300/J101v13n25_11

Primary ①

Introduction

Chapter 1 introduces various primary students (kindergarten to grade three) in the context of Ontario schools, typically within inclusive classroom settings. Case 1 (What's Next for Nora?) is introduced from the point of view of a resource teacher in a busy urban school, focusing on a grade two Indigenous student with Autism Spectrum Disorder (ASD) in a complex family situation who is transitioning to a new school environment. Case 2 (What Does Luc Need?) is written from the point of view of a teacher in her first contract position, beginning with her participation in one of her first IEP meetings—for Luc. Luc is a grade three student identified as "Multiple"—with both a learning disability and an ASD. Case 3 (Getting Ready for Rayna) showcases a teacher in a self-contained classroom preparing her environment for a new grade one student who is moving from kindergarten into a new board, school, and classroom with a range of individualized equipment to support her success. Rayna has a developmental delay and a physical disability. Case 4 (A Query around Scarlett) is explained from the point of view of a board-based teacher consultant for special education. In this case, the consultant is reviewing information about a grade four student who might qualify for an identification of giftedness and communicating by email with her school-based resource teacher. Case 5 (Dana's Transition to School) focuses on same-gender parents transitioning their twins into their first year of kindergarten, including Dana, a young learner with low vision. This case focuses on an in-school team meeting to support effective transitions into school-aged care and education, as well as the development of a new Individual Education Plan.

Each case in Chapter 1 includes a range of brief response questions and in-depth response questions; resources, figures, and templates are included as needed. Integrated into each case are several keywords, which are defined in the margins, as well as in a glossary at the end of the book. Suggested readings, websites, articles, and multimedia are found at the end of the chapter, along with chapter references.

Case 1: What's Next for Nora?

Age 6, Grade 2, I wrote, chewing slightly on the end of my pencil. Our school was about to receive a new student at the end of September. Her **Ontario Student Record** (OSR) had luckily preceded her arrival from her fairly isolated northern school. As the **resource teacher** in my bustling and ever-growing K–6 public school, one of my jobs is always to review OSRs after the principal has had a look. Then, I make note of any issues—or celebrations—and send summaries to all classroom teachers and other involved personnel, if needed, as a start to fully prepare to welcome new students.

Typically, I only do this particular task; however, for students who have **Individual Education Plans** (IEPs), have IEPs in progress, or whose files present any areas of concern when our school administrator views them, my work does not stop here. *In this case, with a fairly slim file, it seems likely be to one of the latter two situations, but time will tell!* Although I wasn't sure, yet, why Nora's OSR was nestled into my mailbox in our staff room, the bright sticky note, *PLEASE REVIEW! ! !* from my principal, written with urgent capital letters and multiple exclamation marks, definitely gave the message that it was necessary, and that the mystery reason would be evident at some point.

Nora, Indigenous, Female, I wrote on my notepad, pulling out what I thought were perhaps essential pieces of information to paint a picture of Nora as an individual student from the now-open file on the desk in front of me, knowing that more important details would emerge as I leafed further into the depths of this OSR. Some notes, however, were more for inside my head than on my notepad—helpful, perhaps, for when I meet Nora's family later this term. I made a mental note that it looks like Nora is part of a single-parent home, headed by her mother as that sole parental figure. *This is not uncommon in our school,* I thought, *with our diverse families that make up our—thankfully—eclectic and accepting student body.* Confirming my hypothesis, I found a copy of a quite recent custody agreement between Nora's biological parents. *It looks like Nora is moving here to this suburban southern Ontario city from northern Ontario, with her mother, and her biological father will be staying behind, keeping in contact with Nora on school holidays. So, this means that Nora's father has limited custody rights, but custody rights nonetheless. It will be important for our school to know this, so we can send out a copy of all report cards, IEPs, and other important school documents.* I made a note of this last detail, and also wrote that Nora would not be joined by any siblings at our school (important for when we send school-wide notices home). It looked like that was the last piece of information about Nora's background beyond her academics, so I slotted in a coloured piece of card stock paper to separate and organize her demographic information for the next professional who comes to seek information about Nora. Before delving into more in-depth details about Nora, I turned over her OSR to get an overview of her schooling experiences—so far—from the chart on the back.

From the dates on the back of the OSR, which listed Nora's schools and teachers, and the lack of any information about kindergarten, it seemed that Nora had not entered the formal school system until her grade one year. There was only one school photo depicting Nora in grade one, posing for the camera with a shy smile, clutching what looked likely to be one of her favourite books. *It's too bad that Nora was not able to take part in the full-day kindergarten that our board offers,* I considered, with visions of our two-year kindergarten programs rich with literacy, numeracy, and social opportunities playing in my head. *Since kindergarten is not compulsory in Ontario, there would be nothing in her record declaring that she was being home-schooled before she turned six.* I concluded that Nora may have been home-schooled or was not formally attending school yet, perhaps, throughout kindergarten and before she turned six, but clearly she entered formal schooling in her grade one year in an **inclusive classroom**.

Flipping back to the inside of Nora's OSR, I found three evaluations—a progress report and two report cards—for Nora's grade one year. None of them noted the presence of an IEP on the checkboxes beside her subject areas; yet, almost every area of Nora's report cards was checked off as "Progressing with difficulty." *Aha— no IEP. Well, I guess that's not the reason that I am reviewing Nora's OSR,* I thought. *I have seen other students struggle with transitions because of curriculum shifts—even the change in what was or was not covered in a given year (so far) in any classroom.* Further pondering, I thought, *And, as a profession, we have to watch out for differentiating between what might be a social need in an unfamiliar context for any one student, versus what might be an exceptionality.*

> **Inclusive classroom**
> A classroom environment where differentiated learning opportunities are created and all students, regardless of ability, can learn and be supported together.

> **Individual Education Plan (IEP) software** Any program that is designed for developing IEPs in an online environment, which allows for access by multiple professionals. The software is designed specific to the policies, procedures, and needs of a specific jurisdiction, such as a school board.

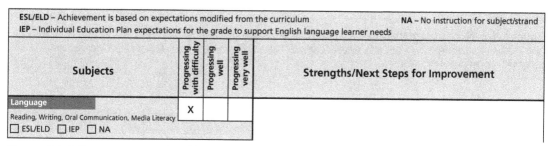

Figure 1.1.1 Progressing with Difficulty
Source: Adapted from Ontario Ministry of Education, 2010. http://www.edu.gov.on.ca/eng/policyfunding/growsuccess.pdf, p. 99.

It looks like I need to put our teachers on alert for potential academic difficulties, too. It is perhaps unfortunate that no referrals have yet been made to support her clearly at-risk status when it comes to academics—especially language. With some questions in my mind, I shut Nora's OSR and rolled my chair a little sideways to log onto the resource room's desktop computer to finish typing my summary of information. As I typed, my concern grew, and so did the feeling that I must have missed something.

I logged into my board's **IEP software** to see if there was an IEP in our board's online IEP system for Nora—with no success. Unable to shake that feeling, I retrieved Nora's file, and again paged through it, carefully rechecking the back pages of each entry. Though I found nothing new, I did find something that looked very well used. There was one slim sheaf of missed papers just inside the back of the OSR's manila folder, partly held in place by a paper clip, but folded almost totally up in an accordion-like manner. *It must have shifted during mailing,* I surmised.

Hoping for a missing piece to the Nora puzzle, I was not disappointed. I unfolded and flattened out what was clearly at least a partial **Statement of Decision**

> **Statement of Decision** A written document developed as an outcome from an IPRC meeting. It includes whether (and under which categories) the IPRC has identified the student as exceptional, the placement decision, recommendations regarding programs or services, the reasons behind the decision, and strengths and needs used to build an IEP (if the student is exceptional).

from an IRPC meeting stapled to some other, potentially illuminating, paper-work. It read:

DECISION OF THE IPRC COMMITEE

☐ The committee recommends that the student is not identified as exceptional according to the definitions outlined in Reg. 181/98 and defined by the Ministry of Education and Training 1998.

☒ The committee recommends that the student meets the criteria for an exceptional student as outlined in Reg. 181/98.

IDENTIFICATION

☐ Behaviour	Communication	Intellectual	Physical	☐ Multiple
	☒ Autism	☐ Giftedness	☐ Physical Disability	
	☐ Deaf and Hard of Hearing	☐ Mild Intellectual Disability	☐ Blind/Low Vision	
	☐ Language Impairment	☐ Developmental Disability		
	☐ Speech Impairment	☐ Learning Disability		

PLACEMENT

☒ Regular class with indirect support   ☐ Special education class with partial integration
☐ Regular class with resource assistance   ☐ Special education class full-time
☐ Regular class with withdrawal assistance

Figure 1.1.2 Nora's (Partial) IPRC: Statement of Decision
Source: Adapted from template, Ontario Ministry of Education, 2004. http://www.edu.gov.on.ca/eng/general/elemsec/speced/guide/resource/iepresguid.pdf, p. 52.

Identification, Placement, and Review Committee (IPRC) Composed of at least three persons, one of whom must be a principal or supervisory officer of the board, the IPRC must decide whether and under what categories students should be identified as exceptional, decide appropriate placement for the student, and review their decision annually. Regulations 181/98 drive this process.

Okay, I summarized in my head, adding to my notes for Nora's teachers. *It looks like Nora was assessed during what would have been her kindergarten year; then she went through the* **IPRC** *process last year. It looks like she was identified as an exceptional student through the* IPRC. *I can see that her identification is listed as* **Communication: Autism.** *So that means she has had, in all likelihood, a medical or clinical diagnosis of* **Autism Spectrum Disorder** *that her mother brought to the committee.*

Because of all of the recent changes in the field of ASD, I searched for its new definition for a review, and found a really good, easy-to-read overview on the web-site of the ***Diagnostic and Statistical Manual,* Fifth Edition** (APA, 2014): https://psychiatry.org/patients-families/autism/what-is-autism-spectrum-disorder?_ga =1.210225747.774096327.1483620004. I also made notes on an overview of the changes, such as that the diagnosis is now called only ASD with no subtypes.

This definition would be just perfect to send out to Nora's teachers, I thought, as I marked the link for later. *This particular identification can be a little confusing for teachers. Our educational definition of Communication: Autism has different wording than the clinical diagnosis of Autism Spectrum Disorder, and uses some confusing language. Since students cannot be identified in the school without a clinical diagnosis first, it is important for teachers to be familiar with both.*

Next, I navigated online to *Special Education: A Guide for Educators* and took a screenshot of the definition to add to my email of resources.

Communication

Autism

A severe learning disorder that is characterized by:

a) disturbances in:
   - rate of educational development;
   - ability to relate to the environment;
   - mobility;
   - perception, speech, and language;

b) lack of the representational symbolic behaviour that precedes language.

Figure 1.1.3 Ministry Definition of Communication Screenshot
Source: Screenshot, Ontario Ministry of Education, 2001. http://www.tncdsb.on.ca/new/resources/ SPED%20A%20Guide%20for%20Educators%2001.pdf, p. A18. © Queen's Printer for Ontario, 2001. Reproduced with permission.

Figure 1.1.4 Effective Educational Practices for Students with Autism Spectrum Disorders Cover
Source: *Ontario Ministry of Education*, 2007a. http://www.edu.gov.on.ca/eng/general/ elemsec/speced/autismSpecDis.pdf, Cover page. © Queen's Printer for Ontario, 2007. Reproduced with permission.

**Communication:
Autism**   Identification used by the Ontario Ministry of Education to describe a severe learning disorder characterized by change in rate of educational development; ability to relate to the environment; mobility; perception, speech, and language; and lack of representational symbolic behaviour that precedes language. It is analogous to the clinical definition of ASD but uses the categories and subcategories of school-based special education.

Autism Spectrum Disorder (ASD)   A complex neurobiological condition that is primarily evident by difficulties in social communication skills and restricted/repetitive behaviours. The use of "spectrum" refers to the continuum of severity, symptomology, and functioning that individuals with ASD exhibit.

Diagnostic and Statistical Manual, Fifth Edition (DSM-5)   Contains a listing of diagnostic criteria for every psychiatric disorder recognized by the Canadian health-care system.

I also added links to some of the other important initiatives in ASD. First, I added the ministry's *Effective Educational Practices for Students with Autism Spectrum Disorders*; then, I included a link to *Policy/Program Memorandum 140: Incorporating Methods of Applied Behaviour Analysis into Programs for Students with Autism Spectrum Disorders* (http://www.edu.gov.on.ca/extra/eng/ppm/140.html).

These are both examples of important resources to support students with ASD in schools, I reflected. I could add many more, but I don't want to overwhelm everyone. While all of them know about ASD, they haven't all taught students identified with ASD—yet.

Saving my email as a draft, I turned over and smoothed the well-worn paper again, finding some illuminating

Assessment summary
Provided by the clinician who completes an assessment, it contains a summary of the results of the assessment as well as suggestions for treatment/intervention.

handwritten notes underneath. *The classroom teacher and the resource teacher must have been in the process of writing up Nora's IEP after all—a job I will be continuing. This will be very helpful information for her **assessment summary**—I will just have to see if I can track down the original reports. It looks like the most recent assessment was done by the resource teacher quite recently: the Woodcock-Johnson Test of Achievement, which showed multiple delays in the standard battery of subtests, meaning that Nora is behind standardized norms areas like letter–word recognition.* I read the list of jot notes:

- Hearing and vision screen showed normal.
- Bayley Scales of Infant and Toddler Development. Showed delays in various areas, including social–emotional, adaptive, cognitive.
- Childhood Autism Rating Scale. Indicated mild autism. Some subtests in the 2nd and 5th percentiles.
- Vineland Adaptive Behaviour Scales. Multiple domains below the 25th percentile. Motor skills highest (10th percentile).
- Conners Rating Scales–Revised (CRS-R™). Clinically significant difficulties with peer relations and inattention.

And these notes, I mused, examining the papers in front of me, *must be from her previous school's in-school team meeting.* I reviewed a list of what I thought must be recommendations, but perhaps only in draft form:

1. Speech and language therapy
2. Strong emphasis on communication and social skills
3. Occupational and physical therapy assessment for fine motor skills
4. Annual pediatric/hearing/vision examination
5. Focus on Applied Behaviour Analysis
6. Needs in (and programs for) communication (expressive/receptive), social skills, language, math (accommodations, modifications, alternate courses)

Interesting, I thought! *Well, I had better finish that email with the recommendation that we should convene our own in-school team, soon, and put Nora on the list. So, I am printing that summary to put in all of Nora's teachers' mailboxes in the staff room. I have a reading list to send with information about ASD, provincial legislation, and some excellent resources. Next on my list is to get going on this IEP. But, first, it's time to make some phone calls home to check in with Nora's parents and see where their priorities lie for her education.* I clicked "Send" on my email, made a note about my phone calls, put Nora's name on my IEPs-in-development list, and took my printed summary about Nora next door to photocopy and distribute. *It looks like we are on our way to supporting Nora at our school in the best possible way.*

Brief Response Questions

1. Who will provide speech and language therapy for Nora? Investigate some details about school-based SLP (speech–language pathologist) services, such as its availability, regularity, and service type (e.g., direct/indirect).
2. Where is information about custody rights and schools available?
3. How does an IPRC identification of an exceptional student relate to the development of the IEP?
4. Is there any relationship between the Ontario's Freedom of Information and Privacy Act and Nora's case?
5. Why was Nora's resource teacher happy to have found additional information in Nora's OSR when she looked again?
6. Why were Nora's parents not consulted in terms of interests, strengths, and/or needs? Briefly discuss and, if relevant, add what you would do differently.
7. If Nora was educated on a reserve up until this point, how might her file have looked different from what the resource teacher received? Respond with reference to policy, practice, and/or legislation.

In-Depth Response Questions

1. Is anything missing from Nora's OSR? If so, describe. If not, describe why it is complete.
2. How might attending kindergarten—especially Ontario's full-day two-year kindergarten—support Nora or another student with special needs? Support your comments with reference to provincial information, such as the *Final Report: Evaluation of the Implementation of the Ontario Full-Day Early Learning Kindergarten Program* (Vanderlee, Youmands, Peters, & Eastabrook, 2012).
3. Describe PPM 140 and the role of Applied Behaviour Analysis (ABA) in Ontario schools. How will this information and/or such services likely be integrated into Nora's future IEP? Explain.
4. Once Nora's IEP is written, explain what will happen next. For example: How often will it need to be updated? What will the roles of the resource teacher, parents, and classroom teacher(s) look like? Who is likely to be the "main author" of any IEP updates? If Nora is identified as an exceptional student, how will this change her IEP? Refer to *The Individual Education Plan: A Resource Guide* in your responses.
5. It is possible that Nora is just learning the English language? If so, explain how this could have impacted her assessments. If not, explain how you know this information from the above case.

continued

6. Ontario's Ministry of Education has committed to an objective that is listed as "encour-
    age more faculties of education and colleges to further enhance the knowledge and skills
    of teacher candidates and teachers in the field to better prepare them to work with First
    Nation, Métis, and Inuit students, including students with special education needs"
    (Ontario Ministry of Education, 2007b, p. 11), yet Nora's resource teacher didn't prioritize
    any related information that she sent to Nora's other teachers. Explain how Nora's resource
    teacher might have approached this information differently.

Figure 1.1.5 Truth and Reconciliation Commission of Canada: Calls to Action Cover
Source: National Centre for Truth and Reconciliation. *Truth and Reconciliation Commission of Canada: Calls
to Action*, 2015. http://www.trc.ca/websites/trcinstitution/File/2015/Findings/Calls_to_Action_English2.pdf,
Cover page.

Case 2: What Does Luc Need?

Let's do this! As a grade three classroom teacher with many years of substitute teaching and Long-Term Occasional contracts in every grade and every school that I could find within an hour of driving from my apartment, but in my first year at a permanent position, I was feeling quite nervous about what was ahead. I was headed into an IEP meeting with some of the other teachers—whose names I am still learning—for a student not new to our school, but new to me. *It's too bad the parents couldn't come today*, I thought. *But I am not sure if that makes me more or less nervous! When we talked about parental roles in our Bachelor of Education classes, it was emphasized over and over that the parents are the experts on their own children, and that* **collaboration** *is one of the foundations of effective home/school communication, especially when it comes to students with* **exceptionalities***. What if we make a decision that the parent doesn't like? What will happen then? What if he needs something I can't provide?*

I headed down to the vice-principal's office, still considering these somewhat anxiety-producing thoughts, where we could easily meet with some confidentiality, and without staff and students walking in and out during after-school extra-curriculars. *That's one thing I have noticed about this school, even when I was substituting here. People actually pay attention to signs on doors! So, I know when they see "Meeting in Progress," they won't walk in, and they probably won't even knock. When we are talking about weighty issues like a student's IEP, I sure don't want to be interrupted!* While walking, I scanned through the list I had made of the contents of the accordion file I was carrying, which included some samples of Luc's in-class work from the first few days of classes this year. It was clear to me (even if I hadn't read Luc's file long before the first day of school) that Luc really struggled with **auditory learning**, as well as with **written expression**.

When I arrived at the VP's office, the resource teacher welcomed me kindly and showed me my seat. Thankfully, she began by introducing the others in the room: the Physical Education teacher and Luc's grade two teacher from last year. "Ms Linna," she addressed me, "we were just chatting about Luc and his success in Physical Education class last year. Would you like to hear what worked?"

"For sure!" I immediately responded, delighted that we weren't just going to talk about problems.

"I wouldn't have believed it," the French teacher began, "but what Luc loves, Luc really loves. At the start of last year, all he could tell me about was how he hated gym class and loved Pokémon. He would repeat this over and over, two or three times per class, every time we had class. So, our wonderful resource teacher here gave me this fantastic book called *Just Give Him the Whale!* It sounds a little over-the-top when I listen to myself say this, but it literally changed our student–teacher relationship, not to mention Luc's Physical Education evaluation! So, it's all about using a student's expertise, for example, to support success. When Luc was in my class, so were the Pokémon. If we were doing warm-downs, his giant stuffed Pokémon were doing them too, with Luc's help. If we were using a ball, Luc or his team used the Pokémon ball. I could go on, but I am sure you get the idea. The

Collaboration
A method where a group of individuals work together to achieve a common goal. Each member's opinion and ideas are viewed as valuable and equal to each other's in a way to formulate solutions to a problem or completion of a task.

Exceptionalities
A word used in education (typically analogous to disability) to broadly describe an individual based on their level of need in relation to the developmental and physical domains for their age. A person is identified as exceptional in specific areas or as an overall learner.

Auditory learning
A learning style in which an individual depends on hearing as a main method of comprehending and retaining incoming information.

Written expression
A complex task requiring the integration of cognitive, linguistic, and motor abilities. Learning disability with impairment in written expression involves the inability to write, primarily referring to handwriting, but also coherence, occurring due to an issue in the brain related to orthographic encoding, not visual or motor impairment.

Identification The process of using gathered information—including work samples, assessment data, observations, and experiences—to categorize students based on their learning needs in order to provide more accurate and focused programming for the students.

Multiple A combination of two or more school-based identifications including learning and other disorders, impairments, or physical disabilities that exist together for one student.

Learning disability (LD) An umbrella term for a wide variety of issues resulting from neurodevelopmental disorders that affect the ability to acquire, retain, understand, organize, and/or use verbal and/or non-verbal information; may be associated with difficulties in social interaction; and are not the result of hearing/vision acuity, intellectual disabilities, socio-economic factors, cultural differences, language barriers, lack of effort, or educational opportunities.

point is, we included that on all the drafts of his IEP moving forward under strengths, and as a teaching strategy in his individualized courses. So far, Luc is sticking with Pokémon, but when he focuses on something else, you better believe we will, too!" (Kluth, 2008).

"That gets us started really well on a positive note. Thank you," responded the resource teacher, allowing me some time to nod thoughtfully and absorb these ideas. "What we want to accomplish in the next hour or so, then, is to go through Luc's IEP that went along with his June report card, and see what needs to be changed or updated. I have some notes here from Luc's parents, and I will be checking in with them, too, after we have a draft made. As you can see at the end of his IEP, in our school, we always make sure that parents are part of the team—in writing. We developed our own IEP template a few years ago, based on one suggested by the Ministry."

"Now, I can deal with all of the updates like Luc's grade, teachers, etc., myself. I see that his first IPRC date was June 19th, 2014. His **identification** is **Multiple**: Autism & **Learning Disability**, and that stays the same, right now. He hasn't had any new formal assessments that we need to add, from the list we have."

"Given that we have already made a start on Luc's strengths, let's update his strengths and needs with anything new."

Figure 1.2.1 Luc's Story on "My Summer Holiday"
Source: Monique Somma (used with permission).

Areas of Strength	Areas of Need
Memorization	Written expression
Mathematics	Social skills
Kinesthetic learning (e.g., Math manipulatives)	Self-regulation skills

Figure 1.2.2 Luc's IEP: Strengths & Needs
Source: Adapted from Ontario Ministry of Education, 2004. http://www.oafccd.com/documents/IEP2004.pdf, p. 52.

IEP developed by: Mrs Doreen Nester (Classroom Teacher), Mrs Lynn Lu (Resource Teacher)

IEP Team Member	Role
Mme Sandy Bogart	French Teacher
Mr Ben Purgit	Vice-Principal
Ms Nellie Tran	Principal
Mr and Mrs Morster	Luc's Parents

Figure 1.2.3 Luc's IEP Team
Source: Adapted from Ontario Ministry of Education, 2004, p. 55.

ASSESSMENT DATA

List relevant educational, medical/health (hearing, vision, physical, neurological), psychological, speech/language, occupational, physiotherapy, and behavioural assessments.

Information Source	Date	Summary of Results
Psychoeducational Report	15 Oct.	"Symptoms indicate a diagnosis of a learning disability that affects written expression."
Audiological Report	9 Apr.	Hearing within normal limits.
Vision Report	4 Dec.	Vision normal. No glasses worn or needed at this time.

Figure 1.2.4 Luc's Assessment Data (Partial)
Source: Adapted from Ontario Ministry of Education, 2004.
http://www.oafccd.com/documents/IEP2004.pdf, p. 52.

Taking advantage of a pause, I jumped in, eager to share my new-found knowledge of Luc. "Well, I think everything you have already listed still mostly applies, but I am pretty sure one thing is missing: his written expression." I showed my collected samples. "Grade three tends to be a turning point when it comes to reading and writing. I think that Luc, from his reports, already has been struggling with writing, but I think he is going to have problems in grade three where we write often and, well, more. While it is really important for Luc to keep working on his skills with a pencil and paper, it's also important for his self-esteem and content knowledge learning to be efficient in his academic work—especially these basic foundations. Has anyone given any thought to assessing, trialing, or teaching Luc about **assistive technology** software?"

"No, not really, actually," responded the resource teacher, with honesty. "It always seems like other areas have been more important to prioritize for Luc. But it is certainly worth doing some trials with **Co:Writer**® or a similar word predic-tion program to see if it helps. It certainly would be a good skill to have, moving along towards junior grades, and since we have so many students using laptops, netbooks, and tablets in our inclusive classes, he will probably be excited about it. We can add on that area of need, and this will be first on my list to discuss with Luc's parents. Maybe we can even get some SEA **funding**. Now, what's next? What else does Luc need this term?"

Assistive technology
Specialized software and/or hardware that adapt how specific tasks can be performed to meet the needs of the user with an exceptionality.

Co:Writer® Word prediction software that allows for text-to-speech capability and enables its users to recognize and select whole words by looking and listening rather than struggling with extensive keyboarding and spelling.

Special Equipment Amount (SEA) funding References any funding for equipment to help accommodate students with special education needs. Students do not have to be formally identified as "exceptional" to qualify.

Brief Response Questions

1. Should Luc be listed as an IEP team member? Why or why not?
2. Why is it likely important to Luc that other students are also using technology in the classroom, such as laptops, tablets, and netbooks?
3. Is anything missing from Luc's assessment list? If so, what? If not, what assessment do you think would be added next? Why?
4. From the below list of Luc's accommodations, sort them into environmental, assessment, and instructional accommodations, as they would appear on an IEP: *high structure, alternate settings, frequent breaks, uncluttered format, oral responses, assistive technology, additional processing time, sensory room, strategic seating, peer tutoring, hands-on manipulatives, verbatim scribing, quiet setting, visual strategies, attention prompts, fewer practice questions, noise-cancelling headphones.*
5. What is one additional way that Luc's teacher could set up the classroom environment for his success? Name, and briefly describe, an appropriate proactive strategy for success.

In-Depth Response Questions

1. It appears that Luc has fairly intensive needs and that his classroom could benefit from the support of an educational assistant (EA). How would Luc's teacher request such support for Luc and her classroom? Explain what procedures she might follow, and support your ideas with at least one board-level or Ministry-level policy, procedure, or document.
2. Using at least one board-level or Ministry-level policy, procedure, or document (e.g., "Special Equipment Amount Funding"), explain how Luc's teacher would initiate a request for SEA funding to support Luc's written expression needs.
3. Name and explain at least three steps in how Luc's teacher would figure out what assistive technology he needs for success in the classroom environment, and who she would need to collaborate with along the way to assess this skill area.
4. Watch an online demonstration of Co:Writer® or another example of AT software (e.g., Google Read&Write), and explain in detail at least two ways that this might help Luc's written expressive language skills.
5. Imagine that Luc's IEP assessment data includes "PM Benchmarks Level 22." How would this help you to plan for his needs? Explain.
6. What are some positive practices to working well with EAs in the classroom environment? List and explain at least three of these strategies. Mounsteven (2010; full reference at the end of the chapter) would be a good place to start your reading.

Case 3: Getting Ready for Rayna

Miss Henning, the teacher of a self-contained classroom for students with developmental disabilities in a large, public, urban school, was readying her classroom for the fall entry of her new students. *It's hard to believe the start of classes is going to be so soon*, she thought. *It still feels like the middle of summer! However, first things first. . . .*

Miss Henning went to the front of her classroom door—already propped open to let in the breeze—and used her fingernails to pry off the engraved chrome strip on her doorway announcing the "Special Education Class." She replaced it with one inscribed with "Miss Henning," peeled off the protective plastic, and tamped it down tightly with the palm of her hand. *There*, she thought with satisfaction. *Now we will be able to tell my class apart from the other so-called special education classes in my school. I would rather have the other students saying, "Are you in Miss Henning's class?" to my students than, "Are you in the special education class?" We have come a long way since doors like mine used to have signs like "Trainable Mentally Retarded" on them. Thank goodness for that! But we still do have a long way to go.*

She picked up her tablet and opened her to-do list app, to check off and then delete this first task accomplished in her classroom readiness. *What's next?* The next task was highlighted in red—as urgent—and was: check over Rayna's equipment. Rayna had just moved over from another board, and her equipment had arrived over the summer, carefully grouped together in the corner of the classroom. Miss Henning found her clipboard where she had printed out a list of Rayna's equipment straight from her spring IEP, so she could be sure that everything was on site for the start of grade one.

Until my principal provided me with information about SEA-funded equipment, Miss Henning reminisced, *I had no idea that equipment like Rayna's would travel from place to place. I thought we were going to have to start at the beginning to set up my classroom for success. It's a good thing that he pointed out to me that this is not the case.* She thought back to her summer reading from the "Special Education Funding Guidelines: Special Equipment Amount" document, found in her school's binder of processes and policies around just such equipment. She had read:

> When a student who uses SEA purchased equipment moves from school to school or board to board, the equipment should move with the student unless, in the opinion of a receiving board, it is not practical or

---

Individualized Equipment   ☑ Yes *(list below)*   ☐ No

Tilt-top desk / book box	*Ergonomic chair (with high armrests)*
Interlocking footrest	*Wiggle chair cushion*

Figure 1.3.1 Rayna's Individualized Equipment List

Source: Adapted from Ontario Ministry of Education, 2004. http://www.oafccd.com/documents/IEP2004.pdf, p. 53.

efficient to move the equipment. The student's sending board will not be reimbursed by the Ministry. The receiving board will be responsible for any shipping or handling costs associated with the timely and effective transfer of equipment. It is expected that a board will transfer a student's equipment within six weeks of receiving a request for the student's equipment from the receiving board. (Ontario Ministry of Education, 2015a, pp. 7–8)

She had also read:

Boards will develop policies and procedures that provide board staff with direction on issues such as
- equipment transfers between schools and between boards;
- use of equipment in student's home, in co-op placements and in other program settings;
- staff training on the use of SEA funded equipment;
- secure storage of equipment;
- timely acquisition and use of equipment; and
- inventory records. (Ontario Ministry of Education, 2015a, pp. 7–8)

Modified courses
Subjects or courses with changes made to the age-appropriate grade-level expectations in order to meet a student's learning needs. These changes may involve using expectations developed for a different grade level and/or increasing or decreasing the number and/or complexity of the regular-grade-level curriculum expectations.

Alternative courses
Subjects developed on a student's IEP to address various aspects of student need that are not specifically represented in the Ontario curriculum, in order for the student to learn new skills. These may include areas such as social skills, communication skills, or money management, depending on individual need. At the high school level, these would not be given formal credits.

I don't mind admitting, actually, that I really enjoyed reading up on this policy, and that I read the whole document! Though I am obviously going to have to keep up to date on it, as it changes from year to year, I did learn quite a few interesting points, like that students do not have to be identified to get funding for SEA equipment. That's pretty exciting!

One by one, Miss Henning peeled the packing tape off Rayna's boxes, and set up her specialized desk, chair, and other individualized equipment.

Next, Miss Henning pulled up Rayna's IEP on her desktop computer, which was linked to the in-school collaborative online software that allowed all Rayna's teachers to view the details of her academic program—and its accommodations. *Okay,* she confirmed, *so I can see that as well as specialized equipment, Rayna also had access to regular support from a board-based Occupational Therapist who will now come to our classroom, it looks like, twice a month, and she also goes to the children's centre to meet with her Physical Therapist, about as often. Now I know what they mean when they keep telling me that we are a "hub" of services here at the school! It looks like, as well, that Rayna spends about half of her time in our classroom, but also spends half of her time in one of the other grade two classes.* Miss Henning could see that the option "Special education class with partial integration" was checked off on Rayna's IEP, and thought, *I must remember to check and see if that grade two class also has her specialized equipment available. Clearly, these are essential items for Rayna's success, since her needs are listed as "fine motor skills" and "gross motor skills"! I can also see that besides accommodations all subjects listed for Rayna are* **modified** *or* **alternative courses***. It looks like I have lots of resources to get ready, so I better keep on keeping on!*

Assessment	Summary of Results
Letter Identification *(identifying letter names in and out of context and sequence)*	12/26
Letter Sound Identification Letter identification *(identifying the correct letter when hearing the sound of the letter)*	24/26
Sound identification *(making the sound the letter makes)*	16/26
Spelling Inventory	8/48
High Frequency SK Word List	5/30
Gates–MacGinitie Reading Test	*Low average score in comprehension; Below average score in vocabulary (accommodations in reading questions; answers were scribed)*
Psychological	*Results consistent with the MOE identification criteria for Developmental Delay General Ability Index – Low (in 1st Percentile)*
PM Benchmark	*Level 0 (Pre-K)*

Figure 1.3.2 Assessment List
Source: Author-generated.

SMART A guide to goal setting. Stands for Specific, Measurable, Achievable, Relevant, and Time-limited.

Universal Design for Learning (UDL) An educational framework to improve and optimize learning based on research in the learning sciences, including cognitive neuroscience, that can accommodate individual learning differences.

Educational assistant Support staff person who may work with students individually or in small groups to deliver activities that reinforce and advance their learning.

Brief Response Questions

1. Would you change the name of this classroom? Why or why not?
2. Create at least one **SMART** goal for Rayna that could be integrated into an alternate course.
3. Find a board-based SEA policy and list any questions you have about it. If you do not have any questions, list some points of interest.
4. How should Miss Henning introduce Rayna to the school and classroom?
5. Rayna has a modified course in Language. What information would you need to develop this course?
6. What is one technique that can be used for teaching behaviour self-regulation? Briefly summarize this strategy.
7. Look up one of the assessments on Rayna's list, and briefly explain the assessment and its results.

In-Depth Response Questions

1. Do some research into the history of labels for people with disabilities. Describe your discoveries in approximately three paragraphs or one page.
2. Miss Henning's classroom needs to be accessible for the needs of Rayna and all her students. Explain how such suitably designed environments fit with the principles framed in **Universal Design for Learning** as described in *Learning for All* (Ontario Ministry of Education, 2013).

continued

3. Does Miss Henning's classroom need the support of an **educational assistant**? Explain why or why not, and, using policy, legislation, and/or practice, discuss whether or not you think that her classroom would be given this support.

4. On Rayna's IEP, her "Areas of Strength" are listed as oral expression and verbal comprehension. Her "Areas of Need" are listed as receptive language (verbal, written), working memory, motor skills (fine, gross), pragmatics, phonemic awareness, behavioural self-regulation, written language, executive functioning, and numeracy. Is it a problem that the areas of need are far longer than the areas of strength? If so, how could you resolve it? If not, why not?

5. Using the below template, develop a modified Language course for one term of Rayna's IEP.

Special Education Program

To be completed for each subject/course with modified expectations and/or each alternative program with alternative expectations.

Student OEN/MIN:	Subject/Course/Alternative Program:

Current Level of Achievement:	Current Level of Achievement for Alternative Program:
Pre-requisite course _____	
Letter Grade/Mark _____	
Curriculum Grade Level _____	

Annual Program Goal(s): A goal statement describing what the student can reasonably be expected to accomplish by the end of the school year in a particular subject, course, or alternative program.

Learning Expectations	Teaching Strategies	Assessment Methods
(List modified/alternative expectations outlining knowledge and/or skills to be assessed, by reporting period. Identify grade level, where appropriate.)	(List only those that are particular to the student and specific to the learning expectations.)	(Identify the assessment method to be used for each learning expectation.)

Figure 1.3.3 Modified program template
Source: Adapted from Ontario Ministry of Education, 2004. http://www.edu.gov.on.ca/eng/general/elemsec/speced/guide/resource/iepresguid.pdf, p. 54.

Case 4: A Query around Scarlett

Mrs Mallabar—Linnea to her colleagues at the school board—sat down at her board office laptop after a busy morning of attending **resource team** meetings at three different schools in her assigned geographical area. As she ate her sandwich, she began the lengthy process of catching up on her email (so far) from the workday. While her fingers automatically clicked the right keys, she reflected on her day so far. *What a treat it is to consult with so many of our schools*, she contemplated. *We have so many dedicated, passionate educators who are watching for red flags and picking up early signs of struggles in the classroom, and who are encouraging individualized assessments to make sure that all the right supports are in place for academic success. I really like how so many of our new educators, as well, are emerging from their professional programs already understanding that assessments and diagnoses are not about labelling and categorizing but about finding a starting place to support individual children and, often, about helping out with additional funding and support opportunities.*

Her attention moved back to the adjacent screen when she scrolled down to an email entitled "Consult re Giftedness??" It was from one of her favourite resource teachers in a K–6 school, a hard-working and highly experienced teacher who had a history of success with junior and intermediate students with challenging problem behaviours, but a strong level of interest in learning about all students on his caseload. Mr Megat often checked in with her about some interesting students when he had exhausted all his on-site resources. Her interest piqued, she opened this email first. She read:

Linnea:

I am hoping you can help me out with this extra-special case. As it is April now, when our school usually conducts our grade-wide screenings for giftedness in grades three and six, I am thinking of nominating one of our newer students, Scarlett, who transferred in from out-of-province. Though she is in grade four and isn't part of the screening, I think that maybe she should be re-assessed. I am just going to tell a bit about her background, while trying not to make this email too long. Perhaps we can follow up with a Skype?

So, I have been talking off and on with Scarlett's teacher this year, and of course I have read Scarlett's file. Basically, she has lived in Ontario, Quebec, Alberta, British Columbia, and Nova Scotia. Her father is a teacher and her mother is a college instructor; she has no other siblings. Her mother's work has taken them all over the country, but it seems like she now has a permanent position here, and Scarlett will be staying at our school long-term. In every school she has attended—that's three schools before us—and even in notes from her preschool, there are both anecdotal and formal indications that she would fit under our identification of Intellectual: **Gifted**.

Resource team A group of individuals working at the school-board level that supports resource teachers and schools in matters that require intervention and support beyond what the school can currently provide for a student. Members may complete more formal assessments, support schools with specialized training, observe students with significant needs and assist in implementing strategies and supports, and liaise with outside agencies.

Gifted An exceptionality characterized by an unusually advanced degree of general intellectual ability that requires a greater breadth and depth of learning experiences in order to satisfy the student's educational potential. High scores on psychoeducational assessments are usually required for entrance into a program but the specific requirements vary by board.

Canadian Cognitive Achievement Test (CCAT) The CCAT is a standardized, norm-referenced group test that measures verbal, quantitative, and non-verbal cognitive abilities for students in kindergarten to grade 12.

Percentile A type of converted score that expresses a student's score relative to his or her group in percentile points. It indicates the percentage of students tested who achieved scores equal to or lower than the specified score. 60th percentile means that 59 of every 100 students in that same group scored lower than that child.

Woodcock–Johnson IV Tests of Achievement One of three components in a normed battery of psychoeducational assessments with a focus on academic performance, especially in Math and Language. Its purpose is to determine individual strengths, needs, performance patterns, and learning problems in order to support future interventions.

For example, I can see that she took the **CCAT** last year and her scores were pretty high. However, they don't really fit how our board defines giftedness (even though she started to attend enrichment classes out-of-province last year).

I have attached a scanned copy of her results.

But before that, there are notes from her preschool that they had attempted to move Scarlett up to a higher-aged group so that she could move along with a group of children with similar skills, but she refused to leave the puzzles and blocks in her group's classroom. Then, her grade one teacher included a note on Scarlett's report card that he would have referred her to their board's self-contained gifted class if she had been able to stay. Maybe she would like ours? Also, she had an achievement assessment done in grade two that put her at the 99.8th **percentile** for many of the academic areas (especially non-verbal ones) included in the **Woodcock–Johnson IV.** They are noted as "very superior." I think that brings you up to speed.

I would really appreciate your input into which way you think we should go. I know that her classroom teacher is on board, and I am sure the parents would be, too. Please get back to me when you have a chance.

Mrs Mallabar scanned the email again, and opened the attachment, which was a scan of Scarlett's CCAT. She read:

Verbal	Quantitative	Non-Verbal	**OVERALL**
8	8	9	9

Note: Reported in stanines

Figure 1.4.1 Scarlett's CCAT Score Summary
Source: Author-created.

She considered: *So, I can see why he is inquiring.* She pulled up the board's policy on giftedness, and reviewed its notes on quantitative scoring; specifically, cognitive assessments. Though it was a now-familiar document, she wanted to be sure.

Along with information about the student's learning characteristics, academic achievement, and anecdotal information from current teachers, the following quantitative cut-off scores must be met from the Canadian Cognitive Achievement Test:

- two subtest measures (verbal, quantitative, or non-verbal) must have a Stanine score of 9; and,
- at least one subtest measure (verbal, quantitative, or non-verbal) must have a Stanine score of >8.

She scanned Scarlett's assessment report and noted a few other items:

- Scarlett was one of a set of twins, carried full term, but the other twin died shortly after birth.
- Scarlett is lactose intolerant.
- She missed many days of school from kindergarten to grade two from ear infections and lung infections, but is currently healthy.
- She is an avid reader, and regularly types stories on the computer.
- A former teacher had indicated: "Her writing is slow and laborious with an emerging mix of upper- and lower-case letters. It appears quite immature when compared with her peers."
- Scarlett is in French immersion but does well in most areas of French- and English-language curriculum.
- She enjoys sports like swimming and soccer, as well as acting in the local theatre, and using computers.
- Scarlett has a great sense of humour and is well liked by adults and peers.

She sounds like a fascinating girl, Linnea mused, looking up from the screen and her notes, and stretching her back and neck. She clicked "Reply," and began to compose a short response.

Thank you for sending me this interesting information. It certainly sounds like she fits the classic definition of giftedness, when we think back to **Renzulli's triad**. In terms of a formal identification of gifted, that is a bit more problematic. As you know, each board takes the definition of giftedness from the Ontario Ministry of Education, interprets it, and sets policy around it, which the IPRC will follow. Because of her two lower subtest scores, she doesn't actually fit our definition of giftedness. But then again, I don't think we have ever had a child with a score profile like her with a 9 overall. Her non-verbal scores must have been really, really high to pull up her overall score. I actually think that we might need to do something else here, which is to change the board's policy to reflect this potential set of outcomes. Other students beyond Scarlett might fit it, too! So, I suggest waiting for an IPRC until we can address this at the board level, but in the meantime, an IEP can be developed focusing on enriching Scarlett's school experiences and making sure we scaffold her potential as a clearly gifted young learner. Let's talk more by phone later this week.

Renzulli's triad Three overlapping spheres, representing the key qualities of creativity, task commitment, and above-average ability, which intersect at the point of giftedness where all three traits are represented.

Mrs Mallabar pressed "Send" and began to scroll down again through the in-box on her board's email account. *What other surprises might today hold?* she wondered, happily—and nervously—anticipating the upcoming challenges of her workday.

Brief Response Questions

1. Why does a school board need a definition of giftedness?
2. What are the issues around school boards having differing definitions for identification of giftedness?
3. What does the term "screening" refer to in this case?
4. Would Mr Megat have needed parental permission to email Mrs Mallabar with this type of child-specific information. Why or why not?
5. What are stanines, and how are they used in the field of special education?
6. Is giftedness a disability, if special educational services are used to support this identification?

In-Depth Response Questions

1. How does the Ontario Ministry of Education define "giftedness"? Describe this definition in your own words with detail. If you have met a student who is identified as gifted, describe how this student fits with the Ministry's definition.
2. How do you feel about the role of standardized assessment in identifying students as exceptional? Explain.
3. Do any of the background items noted by Mrs Mallabar impact what will happen next with Scarlett? Explain.
4. Is it possible or desirable to have an IEP without an identification through the IPRC process? Discuss with reference to policy, practice, and/or legislation, as well as professional experience.
5. Compare the term "gifted" to the term "gifted and talented." Explain with detail.

Case 5: Dana's Transition to School

I knew Year 1 of kindergarten was going to be hard. I knew that learning the school system would be hard. But I didn't know it was going to be gut-wrenchingly hard. Dana's mom put her elbows on the table and stared at the array of papers in front of her, all crying out for her response before Monday. This past spring, she had needed to return to work and, along with her partner, had decided to take a deep breath and enter their three young children into the school system. Dana—three years old at the time—was registered for full-day classes in her first year of kindergarten. Similarly, her twin sister, Sharon, was also registered. She recalled wiping a few tears away as she filled out the paperwork and squeezed her partner's hand extra-tightly. She then asked for a third registration form from the school's secretary and completed it for their not-very-much older sibling—13 months older—who was really ready to start in the second year of the kindergarten program. *The thought of them being in school all day, and being away from me—from us—all day, was so hard. I had thought once that really difficult bump was smoothed away, the most difficult part would be over.*

But Monday was her first school meeting, following the first full week of school. The school had invited Dana's mother to attend what they called an in-school team meeting. The principal had said, "Normally we don't invite parents to these meetings, because we have so many different students to discuss in a short period of time, but we have agreed to extend our meeting a little so that we can focus on Dana for longer, with the both of you. If you could bring any information about Dana that you would like to share, that would be very helpful, like a diagnosis from a clinician, or recommendations from an intervener."

After arranging after-school child care—no easy task—both moms arrived at the school, with a hefty binder in hand. They had looked back through their *Keeping It Together* binder and had just decided it might be best to take the whole binder to share with the school. They were greeted by the school secretary, who smiled kindly and showed them to the chairs set in the hallway outside the resource room. "I will let them know that you are here, but they won't invite you in until they are ready," she explained. "They have a number of different discussions on their agenda, so the door stays shut for privacy. But don't worry—everyone's friendly!" After the secretary left to inform the group of the arrival of Dana's parents, her moms were alone in the hallway, strangely silent after the departure of students for home. They looked at one another, feeling oddly nervous.

"It's just like when we were in trouble with the principal," they smiled together, their nerves getting the better of them. While they waited, they opened Dana's KIT, removed red sticky flags from a pocket folder, and began to flag what they thought was the most important information for the school. *Diagnosis or recommendations*, they kept in mind. There was quite a bit of material to get through, and this kept them busy until the door quietly opened, and the smiling, already well-known face of the principal appeared, inviting them in.

"Welcome back," the principal began, as some teachers moved out of the room, smiling and saying their goodbyes to one another . . . until tomorrow.

Keeping It Together (KIT) A binder with built-in organizational system for children with exceptionalities, and their caregivers, developed by the McMaster Children's Hospital's CanChild research centre.

"Thank you to both of you for coming in together and meeting us. This will really help us start off the school year well, with the right understanding and supports for Dana fully in place, as soon as possible." The principal introduced the others in the room new to Dana's parents, including the itinerant teacher supporting students with visual impairments and/or blindness and the school's resource teacher. "We also invited our other four kindergarten teachers, and the school's half-time music teacher, as they will also be teaching Dana. Because our school is fairly large, we have a number of kindergarten classes and are also lucky enough to have been able to hire a teacher who specializes in music. So the question, now, is how we teach Dana: what is the best way to meet her needs? We are hoping that you can help us with that. As you know, the only background information we have—so far—is Dana's registration form where you checked the box for "special needs" and wrote Dana's diagnosis—severe **accommodative esotropia**—noting that Dana has what appears to be ongoing low vision problems, and is farsighted, but not legally blind, and that she must wear her corrective lenses. As you know from some of our phone calls, we are seeing a struggle with Dana's transition into a group instructional environment like ours. So, let's talk. I understand you are bringing some documentation in to share with our team. And I also want you to know that we understand that these kinds of meetings can be anxiety-provoking, and we are working hard to avoid making either of you—or anyone—uncomfortable."

Dana's parents first put forward a brief one-page summary report from a specialized ophthalmologist that had first diagnosed Dana, and had been providing care for her vision issues since then.

"Thanks for saying that! We are more than a little nervous, but as it sounds like you want, we definitely want to build positive relationships with everyone at school. So we have carefully prepared for today. One of the things we brought with us is a list of recommendations from the consultant that visited the child-care centre that Dana attended two days a week last year, at the recommendation of her pediatrician. Here they are." Dana's moms placed it in the middle of the table, and the educators passed it around with growing interest.

Accommodative esotropia Crossed eyes caused by the extra focusing efforts (called accommodation) of the eyes as they try to see clearly, typically resulting from eyes that are farsighted (hyperopic). A side effect of the accommodative effort can be excess convergence or crossing of the eyes. If a child's eyes cross at an early age, then vision may not develop normally and may be permanently reduced in one eye.

Teaching Recommendations for Dana	
Instruction	• During instructional time, provide Dana with a fidget toy (e.g., squishy ball, textured items, etc.). • Ask Dana to repeat instructions back.
Classroom Daily Structure	• Provide Dana with a visual or tactile schedule which she can keep with her at all times. • If educators have access to technology, load a schedule for Dana that she can listen to. • Use a chart to indicate when Dana successfully completes various parts of her day (e.g., she may receive a point for sitting on the carpet for circle time).
Environment	• Have a designated spot for Dana during group time (e.g., mark her spot with a sticker on the ground). • Co-create a "bird's nest" or safe space in the classroom that Dana can go to if she feels over-excited or upset.

Figure 1.5.1 Teaching Recommendations for Dana
Source: Author-generated.

"Thank you so much! This will really help us to develop Dana's IEP," enthused the resource teacher. "I was hoping to get this started quite soon, as I have time set aside in September and early October to write or update Individual Education Plans. Are you familiar with this process at all? We think your voices are an important part of planning."

Dana's mother noted, "Well, Dana had an IPP in child care, and we actually brought a copy of that for you, too. In child care, a Registered Early Childhood Educator that specialized in inclusion came almost every day that Dana was there and helped out the other educators, Dana, and the children at the centre."

Individual Program Plan (IPP) An individualized goal-based resource developed with child-care staff, parents, and resource consultants for children in child care, designed to help meet both the family's and the child's needs. The IPP can include training for family members and staff, as well as assessments of the child.

Individual Program Plan	
Child's Name: Dana	**Date of Birth:** 23 March
Resource Consultant: Ian Pewter	**IPP Date:** 16 October
Domain: BEHAVIOUR	**Goal:** To support Dana in understanding and following classroom routines.

Strategies to Achieve Goal:	Date:	Comments/Observations:
Create a folder using pictures of Dana modelling expectations (e.g., a picture of Dana sitting on the carpet with her friends). Review this folder with Dana every Monday morning. Establish transitional routines and practise them consistently with Dana (e.g., always have a marked spot where Dana should be on the carpet or in the line when leaving the classroom). Praise Dana and use a reward system (such as a sticker chart) every time Dana meets an expectation independently. Ensure Dana has access to a daily schedule. If Dana is not transitioning to the next task successfully, remind her to check her schedule and repeat instructions clearly.		

Figure 1.5.2 Excerpt from Dana's IPP
Source: Author-generated. Adapted from instructions from Peel Inclusion Resource Services.

Next, they pulled out a note from their pediatrician. "Our pediatrician gave this to us when we told him we had a meeting with the school." The principal looked puzzled, as schools don't typically see prescriptions, but picked up the piece of paper that had obviously been ripped from a prescription pad.

The principal read it aloud, her voice reflecting a little bit of carefully concealed surprise: "Dana needs an EA at school." She turned it over, and back again,

Speech-language pathologist Health professional with the specialized skills and training necessary to provide prevention, identification, evaluation, and treatment of communication and swallowing disorders.

FROM THE OFFICE OF
DR J.J. QUAN, MD
DEVELOPMENTAL PEDIATRICIAN

Dana needs an EA at school.

-Dr Quan, MD

Figure 1.5.3 Dana's Prescription
Source: Author-generated.

Referrals Information submitted, usually by the resource teacher, to obtain specialized services, equipment, assessments, or treatments for a specific student requiring additional support. Each school board in Ontario varies on how referrals are completed at the school level; however, all requests for additional services must go to the board office for approval.

Behaviour assessment Aimed at verifying the behavioural needs of an individual. A common tool in Ontario is *The Child Behaviour Checklist* by Achenbach and Edelbrock.

Psychoeducational assessment A measure of the academic and cognitive competencies of children; categories of assessments administered include memory, planning, organization, writing, mathematics, and reading. These assessments are used to guide instruction and involve gathering developmental, family, school, social/emotional, personality/temperament, and health histories, and are administered or supervised by a psychologist.

and then placed it carefully in front of her, smoothing out its edges. "Unfortunately," she responded, choosing her words with caution, "physicians don't have jurisdiction in how school support services are prioritized—I mean—they don't get to direct how EA time is used, but I am glad you have brought up this issue. I am already in the process of requesting more EA time for our school, and, in the meantime, I have moved around some schedules so that there is an EA in Dana's classroom at least half of the day for now. I think that's a reasonable start while we work to re-prioritize support time within the school."

"The other topic we wanted to discuss with you," noted the resource teacher, "is Dana's behaviour. Many of our students new to kindergarten and especially those who have never attended any form of formal child care tend to struggle with the transition to the expectations of group instruction, but Dana seems to be having quite a bit of difficulty beyond what we usually see. Now that you have told me that she has also attended preschool, I am a little more worried. She is having trouble sitting still when asked, listening to even brief group lessons, and following one-step instructions. She will often run across our classroom and attempts to run out of the classroom if the door is open, and she seems to really enjoy being chased. Of course, the first thing we are concerned about is her safety, especially where she doesn't have great vision acuity. And, as you know, problem behaviour always has a function, a message—a reason—that we need to find out in a systematic way."

Dana's mothers' mutually widened eyes met across the table. "We must admit that we are surprised to hear this one. We don't have a lot of trouble at home, but our home life is highly structured, as this is the only way to survive with two jobs and three very young children. But the **speech-language pathologist** that used to come to child care told us that we might see some social or behaviour issues emerging in the future. She said that both Dana's speech and her language development are a little below average for her age: I am sure you have noticed that she has some articulation difficulties. We are working on trying to find some private therapy for her but we are not quite there yet. But the SLP did give us a report and it's only a few months old. I guess we should add this one to the pile."

"Thank you so much for all of this information. With your permission," the resource teacher looked at Dana's mothers for confirmation, "we will copy these to put in Dana's file, and use them to develop the first draft of her IEP, and then send the originals back to you. I know that you want to spend some time with our visual itinerant teacher, but before we leave you to that, I think that we should see how things go, and, in the future, we should probably talk about putting in **referrals** to the school board for a **behaviour assessment** and a **psychoeducational assessment**—we currently have a two-year waiting list—as well as sending Dana to the Identification, Placement, and Review Committee (IPRC) for formal identification as an exceptional student. Typically, we don't do this so early, but I think Dana fits well into the provincial classification of **Blind and Low Vision**. In the meantime, you have a great team of educators here to support you." As the team departed, Dana's mothers reached across the table and grasped one another's hands, feeling concerned, but also relieved. *It is good to know that we won't be doing this alone.*

Blind and Low Vision
Formal category of an exceptionality that falls in the category of "physical," as identified by an IPRC; a diagnosed medical condition involving the inability or reduced ability to see.

Brief Response Questions

1. What are two complexities that might exist in the relationships between home and school when multiple siblings enter the school system together?
2. Why do you think that parents are not regularly invited to in-school team meetings, in this scenario?
3. What is one essential change you would make to the school's registration form for parents of children with special needs?
4. Why would a child in kindergarten have an IEP so quickly?
5. Do you think a referral to a behaviour specialist is necessary? Why or why not?
6. What problems might there be with the use of a sticker chart?
7. How might the first-then strategy (or Premack Principle) be helpful for Dana and Dana's educators?

In-Depth Response Questions

1. Dana's IEP would include a transition plan. Find Policy/Program Memorandum 156 and summarize it. Then, find, summarize, and compare a recent board-based policy around transition planning.

continued

2. Using the below template, write a transition plan for Dana, including at least three to five areas of responsibility for transitioning from Year 1 of kindergarten to Year 2.

Transition Plan

Student's name: _____ OEN/MIN: _____

Specific Goal(s) for Transition to _____ Year 2 of Kindergarten _____

_____

_____

_____

_____

Actions Required	Person(s) Responsible for Actions	Timelines

Figure 1.5.4 Transition Plan

Source: Ontario Ministry of Education, 2004. http://www.edu.gov.on.ca/eng/general/elemsec/speced/guide/resource/iepresguid.pdf, p. 57. © Queen's Printer for Ontario, 2004. Reproduced with permission.

3. Access and explore *Shared Solutions* (Ontario Ministry of Education, 2007d), and find some information that could apply to Dana, her parents, and the school staff. Share a related plan for moving forward.

4. Kindergarten is optional in Ontario schools. Find legislation to support this, and indicate if you think Dana should attend kindergarten from two points of view (e.g., parent, teacher, principal, Dana, etc.).

5. Is it possible for problem behaviours to be present in one setting and not another? Research and explain, and apply your findings to the case of Dana.

6. *Mind the Gap: Inequality in Ontario's School's* (People for Education, 2013) notes that "each step in the [support] process can involve delay. Principals report waiting lists for assessment, IPRC meetings, and provision of services. In all, an estimated 38,000 Ontario students are on special education–related waiting lists." This publication also stipulates that most of this waiting is assessment-related, citing one principal's voice as emphasizing that "we desperately need psychoeducational assessments to be completed faster" (p. 21). How might a three-year wait for assessment and/or services affect Dana's future?

Suggested Resources

College of Audiologists and Speech-Language Pathologists of Ontario
http://www.caslpo.com/

Co:Writer® Demo
http://donjohnston.com/cowriter/#.Vj3uD3uVhco

DSM-5 **Diagnostic Criteria**
http://www.autismspeaks.ca/about-autism/diagnosis/dsm-5-diagnostic-criteria/

Early Learners in Preschool/Kindergarten
https://www.youtube.com/channel/UCWP2DOhtShkVSmo5T8hfcBA

Freedom of Information and Protection of Privacy Act
http://www.ontario.ca/laws/statute/90f31

Highlights of Regulation 181/98
http://www.edu.gov.on.ca/eng/general/elemsec/speced/hilites.html

IEP Engine
http://www.iepengine.com

(The) Individual Education Plan: A Resource Guide
http://www.edu.gov.on.ca/eng/general/elemsec/speced/guide/resource/iepresguid.pdf

(The) KIT: Keeping It Together
http://canchild.ocean.factore.ca/en/research-in-practice/the-kit

Learning Disabilities Association of Ontario
http://www.ldao.ca/

Learning for All
http://www.edu.gov.on.ca/eng/general/elemsec/speced/LearningforAll2013.pdf

(The) Ontario Association of Speech-Language Pathologists and Audiologists
https://www.osla.on.ca

Ontario Federation of Indigenous Friendship Centres
http://www.ofifc.org/

Ontario First Nation, Metis, and Inuit Education Policy Framework
https://www.edu.gov.on.ca/eng/indigenous/fnmiFramework.pdf

Ontario Ministry of Education Funding
https://www.edu.gov.on.ca/eng/policyfunding/funding.html

(The) Ontario Student Record Guidelines
http://www.edu.gov.on.ca/eng/document/curricul/osr/osr.pdf

Pearce, L. (2008). Ministry initiatives and what they mean for you. *Autism Matters, 5*(1).

Peel Inclusion Resource Services Model
https://keywestvideo.wistia.com/medias/vpwgp1g8pn

Program/Policy Memorandum No. 140
http://www.edu.gov.on.ca/extra/eng/ppm/140.html

Read&Write for Google Chrome™: Quick Reference Guide
https://www.texthelp.com/Uploads/MediaLibrary/texthelp/US-Training-Documents/
   Read-Write-for-Google-Chrome%E2%84%A2-Quick-Reference-Guide-June-2016.pdf

Shared Solutions (Ontario Ministry of Education)
http://www.edu.gov.on.ca/eng/general/elemsec/speced/shared.pdf

Special Equipment Amount Funding
https://www.edu.gov.on.ca/eng/funding/1516/2015_16SEA_GuidelinesEN.pdf

Teachers' Gateway to Special Education (Ontario Teachers' Federation)
http://www.teachspeced.ca/
http://www.teachspeced.ca/iprc

Teaching the Gifted
http://professionallyspeaking.oct.ca/march_2012/features/teaching_the_gifted.aspx

(The) Truth and Reconciliation Commission of Canada: A Call to Action
http://www.trc.ca/websites/trcinstitution/File/2015/Findings/Calls_to_Action_
    English2.pdf

References

American Association for Pediatric Ophthalmology and Strabismus. (2015). *Accommodative esotropia*. http://www.aapos.org/terms/conditions/9

APA. (2014). *Diagnostic and Statistical Manual of Mental Disorders (DSM–5)*. http://www. dsm5.org/Documents/Autism%20Spectrum%20Disorder%20act%20Sheet.pdf

Autism Canada. (2016). *What is autism?* http://autismcanada.org/about-autism/

Basepoint Solutions Inc. (n.d.). *IEP engine*. http://www.iepengine.com/

Bennett, S., Dworet, D., & Weber, K. (2013). *Special education in Ontario schools* (7th ed.). St. David's, ON: Highland Press.

Bridges Canada. (2014). *Co:Writer® universal*.

CanChild. (2015). *The KIT: Keeping it together*. http://canchild.ocean.factore.ca/en/ research-in-practice/the-kit

Don Johnson Incorporated. (2014). *Co:Writer® universal*. http://donjohnston.com/ cowriter-7/#.Vj7VjHuVhcp

Kluth, P. (2008). *Just give him the whale! 20 ways to use fascinations, areas of expertise, and strengths to support students with autism*. Baltimore, MD: Brookes Publishing.

Kostelnik, M.J., Soderman, A.K., & Whiren, A.P. (2004). *Developmentally appropriate curriculum: Best practices in early childhood education* (3rd ed.). Columbus: Pearson, Merrill Prentice Hall.

Learning Disabilities Association of Ontario. (2015). http://www.ldao.ca/introduction-to- ldsadhd/articles/about-lds/dysgraphia-the-handwriting-learning-disability/

Mounsteven, J. (2010). Educational assistants in Ontario schools. *Autism Matters, 7*(4). http://www.autismontario.com/client/aso/ao.nsf/web/NewsLink

Nelson Education Ltd. (2014). *Woodcock-Johnson IV preview*, Winter(1). http://www .assess.nelson.com/pdf/WJIV15A.pdf

New Brunswick Department of Education. (2007). *Gifted and talented Students: A resource guide for teachers*. http://www2.gnb.ca/content/dam/gnb/Departments/ed/pdf/K12/ Inclusi n/GiftedAndTalentedStudentsAResourceGuideForTeachers.pdf

(The) Ontario Association of Speech-Language Pathologists and Audiologists. (2010). *What is a speech-language pathologist?* https://www.osla.on.ca/en/ SpeechLanguagePathologist?mid=ctl00_LeftMe u_ctl00_TheMenu-menuItem000

Ontario Ministry of Education. (2000). *The Ontario student record guideline.* http://www. edu.gov.on.ca/eng/document/curricul/osr/osr.pdf

Ontario Ministry of Education. (2001). *Special education: A guide for educators.* https:// www.edu.gov.on.ca/eng/general/elemsec/speced/guide/specedhandbooke.pdf

Ontario Ministry of Education. (2004). *The individual education plan: A resource guide.* Toronto, ON: Queen's Printer for Ontario. http://www.edu.gov.on.ca/eng/general/ elemsec/speced/guide/resource/i presguid.pdf

Ontario Ministry of Education. (2007a). *Effective educational practices for students with autism spectrum disorders: A resource guide.* http://www.edu.gov.on.ca/eng/general/ elemsec/speced/autismSpecDis.pdf

Ontario Ministry of Education. (2007b). *Ontario First Nation, Metis, and Inuit education policy framework.* https://www.edu.gov.on.ca/eng/indigenous/fnmiFramework.pdf

Ontario Ministry of Education. (2007c). *Policy/program memorandum 140: Incorporating methods of applied behaviour analysis into programs for students with autism spectrum disorders.* http://www.edu.gov.on.ca/extra/eng/ppm/140.html

Ontario Ministry of Education. (2007d). *Shared solutions.* http://www.edu.gov.on.ca/eng/ general/elemsec/speced/shared.pdf

Ontario Ministry of Education. (2010). *Elementary progress report.* http://www.edu.gov. on.ca/eng/document/forms/report/card/EPR_Public 06.pdf

Ontario Ministry of Education. (2013). *Learning for all.* http://www.edu.gov.on.ca/eng/ general/elemsec/speced/LearningforAll203.pdf

Ontario Ministry of Education. (2014). *Policy/program memorandum 8. Identification and planning of programs for students with learning disabilities.* http://www.edu.gov.on.ca/ extra/eng/ppm/ppm8.pdf

Ontario Ministry of Education. (2015a). *Special education funding guidelines: Special equipment amount.* https://www.edu.gov.on.ca/eng/funding/1516/2015_16SEA_ GuidelinesEN pdf

Ontario Ministry of Education. (2015b). *Highlights of regulation 181/98.* http://www.edu. gov.on.ca/eng/general/elemsec/speced/hilites.html

Ontario Teachers' Federation. (2016). *Teachers' gateway to special education: Alternative IEP programming.* http://www.teachspeced.ca/alternative-iep-programming

Pathstone Mental Health. (n.d.). *Psychoeducational assessments.* http://www. pathstonementalhealth.ca/services/psycho-educational-assessments

People for Education. (2013). *Mind the gap: Inequality in Ontario schools.* http://www. peopleforeducation.ca/wp-content/uploads/2013/05/annual-report-2013-WEB.pdf

Special Needs Opportunity Window. (2013). *Assistive technology: What is assistive technology?* http://www.snow.idrc.ocad.ca/content/inclusive-technology

(The) Truth and Reconciliation Commission of Canada. (2015). *Calls to action.* http:// www.trc.ca/websites/trcinstitution/File/2015/Findings/Calls_to_Action_English2.pdf

Vanderlee, M.L., Youmands, S., Peters, R., & Eastabrook, J. (2012). *Final report: evaluation of the implementation of the Ontario full-day early-learning kindergarten program.* educ.queensu.ca/sites/webpublish.queensu.ca.educwww/files/files/Research/SPEG/ SPEG%20Full%20Day%20Early%20Learning%20Kindergarten%20Report.pdf

Junior (2)

Introduction

Chapter 2 shares stories around a range of junior-aged students (grades four to six) in the context of Ontario schools, mostly in inclusive classrooms. Case 1 (The Resource Team) centres on a resource team meeting in a rural area, gathering together school-based professionals to discuss—and plan for—various students with exceptionalities. Grade four student Alina (labelled with Autism Spectrum Disorder, Developmental Coordination Disorder, and Mild Intellectual Delay) emerges as a focal point of discussions, and first steps for Alina's entry into her new school are planned. Case 2 (Max's Behaviour) focuses on Max: a grade five student with some problem behaviours likely related to prenatal alcohol exposure. Max's teachers find him exhausting and quite contrary, but they work together with the school's principal to make plans for teaching Max some positive social skills to help him with adult interactions at school. Case 3 (Cassalena's Pathway) is framed around the efforts of Mrs Ikeda, her grade five teacher, to decrease Cassalena's behaviours that are interfering with her learning at school, and the supports from multiple interagency professionals to help her learn new skills—and to plan for success. Case 4 (Vanessa's Bully) describes the social impact of peer stigmatizing around Vanessa, a grade four student with Down Syndrome. Vanessa, her family, and her school discover and deal with bullying, and explore the possibilities around restorative justice. Case 5 (Ms Ikeda's Relaxation Station) describes the processes of setting up a relaxation station zone for emotional self-regulation and all the resources and procedures that accompany it (in a grade six/seven class).

Each case in Chapter 2 includes a range of brief response questions and in-depth response questions; resources, figures, and templates are included as needed. Integrated into each case are a range of keywords, which are defined in the margins, as well as in a glossary at the end of the book. Suggested readings, websites, articles, and multimedia are found at the end of the chapter, along with chapter references.

Case 1: The Resource Team

Developmental Coordination Disorder
A motor skills–based disorder in which a delay in the development of motor skills or coordination, rather than an identifiable medical or neurological explanation, results in a child being unable to perform common, everyday tasks.

Mild Intellectual Delay (MID) A learning disorder characterized by lower than normal intellectual development (Intelligence Quotient typically in the 70 to 80 range), with the ability to learn in a regular class with considerable curriculum modification and supportive services; potential for independent social adjustment and economic self-support.

The school's resource team was settled around the table—at least, those who were present. The vice-principal (highly involved with the school's special education services) sat fairly comfortably at the far edge of the table, responding to emails on her laptop while she waited to be able to address her long list of concerns with their interdisciplinary group, committed to supporting their students with the best services available to them. It was getting late. *1:20 already. We were supposed to begin at 1:00 this afternoon.* Although frustrating for these busy professionals, it was also understandable. In fact, it was not an unusual pattern in their geographically large school board, which often seemed rife with many significant student issues. Though they were a quite small school, they were nestled within an area with wide boundaries, making travel time for board-based personnel an ongoing challenge, especially in the winter months.

They were still waiting for the board's social worker, psychologist, and speech-language pathologist: all invaluable members of the team. A few minutes later, the resource teacher asked, "Should we begin?" The others nodded their approval, knowing they could save some of their more complex questions for the arrival of their board-based team members. "I know we have a long list of students to discuss today," he started, nodding at the handwritten list upon which his hands were resting, "but I think that we should start with Alina." Following more nods, he continued. "Alina is going to be a new student to our school. She is going to be in grade four—she is nine years old—but I think we need to make some careful plans for her transition. Many of you will know her father, Mr Best, from some of the engineering projects he has been involved with around town. Alina had been living with her mother and two sisters about four hours south of here. Very unfortunately, her mother and sisters passed away in a car accident about three years ago now." They paused, respectfully, to let this tragedy unfold in their minds. "Alina then lived with her aunt, but she is now on her way to reunite with her father, who has regained custody of her. So, this is likely going to be a tough transition, with lots of need for social–emotional support. Let's talk about that, though, when our social worker arrives. I think she will have some good ideas for supporting Alina's entry into our school. I have also been told that," he looked down, consulting his list, "she has been diagnosed with Autism Spectrum Disorder and **Developmental Coordination Disorder**, and has a **Mild Intellectual Delay**. There are some other issues, as well, but it is sufficient, perhaps, to say that she is a complex child with complex needs."

They decided to continue to discuss other students while awaiting their other team members, and, for the moment, Alina and her needs took a temporary back seat to other issues ongoing at Aurora Borealis Public School. With the rush of information, however, and with the lack of a prompt return to Alina's case when the other team members did not appear, before they knew it, the bell rang to end the day, files were returned to bags, and goodbyes were said. Likewise, the vice-principal picked up her files and her laptop, transferred them to the desk in her own office, and settled in to follow up on her lengthy to-do list.

ELEMENTARY STUDENT REGISTRATION FORM
CONFIDENTIAL

STUDENT INFORMATION		
Legal Surname *Best*	Given Name *Alina*	Middle Name *Ann*
Preferred Surname *Best*	Usual Name *Alina*	

Birthday Month Day Year *June* *10* *2007*	Gender Male (Female)

Grade level at previous school *4*	Previous school name *King Street Public School*	Previous school address *110 King Street South, Salsbury, ON*

Student Address   Street number and name   Apt. *3114 Winegate Drive*

City *Windermere*	Province *Ontario*	Postal Code *G6H 5L6*

Home Phone Number *701 444 5676*	Cell Phone Number *701 323 7788*	Email Address *Besteng75@buzzmail.com*

IPRC Information

Has the student been identified as exceptional through the Identification, Placement and Review Committee IPRC?

(Yes)   No   If yes, please specify

MULTIPLE (Autism, MID)

Does the student have an IEP?   (Yes)   No

HEALTH INFORMATION

Has your child had any ongoing health problems? Please check all that apply

__ Ear Infection	__ Blind/Low Vision	__ Food Allergies	__ Wheelchair
__ Deaf/Hard of Hearing	__ Wears Glasses	__ Insect Sting Allergies	__ Walker
__ Wears Hearing Aid	__ Diabetes	__ Asthma	__ Crutches
__ Heart Trouble	__ Convulsions	__ Other Allergies	__ Service Animal
		__ Anaphylactic	

Epinephrine Auto Injector: Yes   (No)

Does your child have any other medical problems or special educational needs of which the classroom teacher/school nurse or transportation provider should be aware?   (Yes)   No

If Yes, please describe in detail. *Alina has been diagnosed with Developmental Coordination Disorder*

Figure 2.1.1 Alina's Registration Form
Source: Author-generated.

The resource teacher was walking down the hall towards the vice-principal's office.

"This is perfect!" smiled the school's administrative assistant as she approached, and then entered the office with the resource teacher. "I was just about to find the two of you. We have a new student here to register. Alina is here with her dad—he says that you will be all ready for her!" She handed the written registration form to the vice-principal. "I have already made a copy for her file—when it gets here."

Introductions were given and received and both the resource teacher and the vice-principal accompanied Alina and Mr Best on a tour of the school, including—of course—the two grade four classrooms (one grade four classroom and one combined grade four/five classroom).

"Which one will Alina be in?" Mr Best asked as they walked back towards the school's office area.

"Mr Best," responded the vice-principal, "we are not quite sure yet. To be honest, we weren't expecting to see you two quite yet, so we have a plan to solidify our decisions tonight after school."

"Yes, we are very happy to see both of you, though," interrupted the resource teacher, gently. "We are just not sure yet that we know everything about Alina's needs, and we want to be sure her experience is going to be the best one possible. We know that your family has already been through quite enough, and we want this to be a very positive, easy transition."

"Well," said Mr Best, pulling out his electronic scheduler, "I can only give you until Friday. Or Monday. Monday at the latest. I have a new project starting and Alina needs to be in school. What do you need from me to make this happen?" Mr Best spoke bluntly and stood still, his hand gently resting on Alina's shoulder.

"Why don't we continue this conversation in my office?" suggested the vice-principal to Mr Best and Alina. "I have a large basket of books and an iPad with educational games on it. Perhaps Alina would like to use those for a few minutes? What do you think, Alina?"

Alina did not respond verbally, but grabbed her father's hand and pulled on it, as if to hurry him along, flapped her other hand up by her shoulder, and rose to the balls of her feet, bouncing repetitively. "I think that's definitely a YES," laughed her father. "Alina doesn't say much, but she is very easy to understand."

Several days after that first visit, Alina's needs came again to mind on a busy Wednesday. The vice-principal had been watching carefully for the mail and the courier, but no information had yet arrived about Alina. Furrowing her brow with concern, she picked up all the papers and files on her desk, looked on, under, and through them, and leafed through her in-box of follow-up items. However, she was unable to find that carefully written list of Alina's needs, transcribed from a conversation with the resource teacher at Alina's current school. Highly concerned, she checked her mail cubby where she found her long, annotated list from the principal. Attached to the list was a sticky note that indicated, "I found this on the bottom of my file pile on my desk. I thought you would be happy to see it again," initialled by the resource teacher.

Notes—Alina (Grade 5)

- ASD
- Requires support with most activities in class and out of class, academic and social
- Right now has shared support in the classroom with 3 other students although her needs are the most significant
- Is mostly happy while at school although recently has had some emotional outbursts (perhaps due to the anticipated transition??)
- Assessments from the past few years:
  - Speech Language—showed mild phonological delay, delay in receptive and expressive language and phonological awareness
  - Occupational Therapy—fine motor and manual dexterity needs
  - Diagnosis of Developmental Coordination Disorder
- All areas of Math and Language are modified (two grade levels below)
- Benefits from peer supports in the classroom and at recess
- Benefits from scheduled sensory breaks throughout the day

Figure 2.1.2 Principal's Notes about Alina
Source: Author-generated.

With relief, she picked it up, and then checked the courier bag, not expecting anything new. However, today was indeed a great day to finally put plans in place for Alina's imminent arrival. Her Ontario School Record had arrived, including— she quickly looked—a psychoeducational report and a list of needs from Alina's previous in-school team. Feeling much better about supporting Alina's needs well—right from the start—she asked the resource teacher to come to her office to continue putting supports for Alina into place.

In-School Team Recommendations (May):

1. Inclusive classroom
2. Continue support with speech-language, occupational, and physical therapies with semi-annual updates
3. Request updated community assessment to facilitate IEP transition planning
4. Check with father on annual pediatric examination
5. IEP Development—Reading, Writing, and Mathematics require curriculum modifications and accommodations
6. Alternative programming on IEP for Communication and Social Behaviour

Figure 2.1.3 In-School Team Recommendations (Grade Three)
Source: Author-generated.

Psychoeducational Assessment (Grade 4):

It is necessary to identify Alina as exceptional with a Mild Intellectual Disability based on the following assessment scores: verbal comprehension—11th percentile; perceptual reasoning—7th percentile; working memory—4th percentile; processing speed skills—1st percentile. Math and Language achievement scores are below the 2nd percentile.

Figure 2.1.4 Excerpt from Alina's Psychoeducational Assessment (Grade Four)
Source: Author-generated.

IDENTIFICATION

□ Behaviour	Communication	Intellectual	Physical	□ Multiple
	☒ Autism	□ Giftedness	□ Physical Disability	
	□ Deaf and Hard of Hearing	☒ Mild Intellectual Disability	□ Blind/Low Vision	
	□ Language Impairment	□ Developmental Disability		
	□ Speech Impairment	□ Learning Disability		

PLACEMENT

□ Regular class with indirect support	□ Special education class with partial integration
☒ Regular class with resource assistance	□ Special education class full-time
□ Regular class with withdrawal assistance	

Figure 2.1.5 IPRC Statement of Decision (Grade 3)
Source: Adapted from IPRC Statement of Decision, Niagara Catholic District School Board, form F-9.

Brief Response Questions

1. What steps could the vice-principal have taken to avoid losing her list of essential points of information about Alina? Or, why do you think this principal did not choose an electronic note-taking option?
2. What is the most recent piece of legislation around developing transition plans for Ontario IEPs?
3. Explain two additional methods the school could use to make this transition easy and/or positive for Alina and her family.
4. What did Alina's father mean when he said, "Alina doesn't say much, but she is very easy to understand"?
5. What is one additional item that the resource teacher might find in Alina's OSR that could help her plan for Alina's needs? Name and describe it.
6. What limitations exist for IPRC identifications transferring from board to board?

continued

In-Depth Response Questions

1. Should the school administrators have immediately contacted Alina's family by phone around her transfer into the school? Why or why not? If so, what should these pre-conversations have entailed?
2. Was it acceptable for the school to defer Alina's arrival? If so, why? If not, why not? Explain in detail, with reference to legislation, policy, and/or practice.
3. What four points would you add to Alina's IEP; specifically, to help with the development of her transition plan?
4. Research historical legislation in Ontario around transition planning in IEPs. Find at least two changes that have happened since 1980, and describe each of these changes.
5. Research some possible options for improving communication between Alina and her teachers in the school environment, keeping in mind that, typically, a speech-language pathologist assesses and prescribes communication systems.
6. Develop an alternative course in Social Behaviour for Alina. Include at least three **SMART** objectives for her one-term course.

ELEMENTS OF A SMART IEP

1. Assessed strengths and needs are addressed throughout the document.
2. Accommodations listed are individualized to meet the needs of the learner.
3. Current level of achievement is obtained from the previous year's report card and/or current assessment data. The source for the current level of achievement is identified.
4. The annual program goal is observable, measurable, and attainable by the end of the school year/semester.
5. The specific learning expectations break down the annual goal into achievable steps and are written in SMART format.
6. The number of learning expectations per strand and/or subject-specific plan vary depending on the strengths and needs of the student. It has been recommended to in-school teams that concentrating on fewer expectations at a time will generally be more successful.
7. Assessment methods and teaching strategies are specific to the learning expectations.
8. Assessment methods utilize common board assessments (e.g., PM Benchmarks, CASI, PRIME Math, Ontario Curriculum Document rubrics, Ontario Curriculum exemplars, etc.) or what is most appropriate (e.g., behaviour tracking, work samples, etc.).
9. The initial IEP, as well as subsequent updates, are developed in collaboration with the in-school team and parent(s)/student.
10. The IEP is updated each reporting period and changes are made in collaboration with parent(s)/student. Parents can ask for an IEP review by contacting their in-school team.
11. IEPs are meant to be updated on an ongoing basis, based on the success of the plan. Expectations will change as progress is measured.

Figure 2.1.6. Elements of a SMART IEP
Source: Simcoe County District School Board, 2009.

SMART A guide to goal setting. Stands for Specific, Measurable, Achievable, Relevant, and Time-limited.

7. This team is clearly not relying on technology for collaboration when face-to-face meetings might be a challenge. Should they be doing so? Why or why not?

8. What are three possible next steps for a school administrator who is not yet well versed in Ontario special education?

9. There was no discussion about an educational assistant part or full day for Alina. Based on Alina's needs, might there be a case for one? Please outline a rationale for or against an EA, based on the student's needs.

Case 2: Max's Behaviour

"You need to do this!"
"No!"
"You need to—it's your job."
"No way!"
"I need you to do this for me."
"Not a chance."
"Your friends are waiting, I am sure."
"Nope."

This heated and circular exchange between grade five student Max and his very caring and passionate grade five teacher might have continued, but luckily the school's principal, who happened to walk by on his way to the pods of portables behind St Mary Catholic School, interrupted and broke up the ongoing, fruitless struggle. "What's up?" he inquired benignly, as he stopped beside the two, who were standing just outside the door of the grade five classroom, facing one another, both pairs of shoulders squared.

The teacher looked at him with a clear message of "HELP NEEDED" written on her face. "Well, we are just struggling right now. Max is having a lot of trouble with the idea of going out for recess today. The bell rang—I don't know—quite a few minutes ago, and I found him coming out of the bathroom and back into the classroom."

"I see," noted Mr Pawley. "It sounds like he is also struggling with listening to his teacher. Max, are you having a bad day?"

"Pretty much," Max quickly answered back, now leaning against the wall, slumped over and fiddling with some small bit of paper he had found in his pocket.

"Well, how about you head outside now, so you and I don't have to go and have a talk, and then come and see me right after recess. I have a project I am putting together in the front hallway and I could use your help."

"Kay," mumbled Max, who tossed down his scrap of paper and ambled outside, head down.

Max's teacher breathed deeply. "Thank you," she said, "I wasn't getting anywhere. I know I haven't been teaching that long—just a few years—but he is really hard to manage. It seems like, whatever trouble is going on, Max is right in the middle of it. Quite literally. And he can argue impressively well. I don't know if it's because his parents are both lawyers. Maybe he is angry because he was adopted? But I can never get the upper hand with him."

"Well, come and see me after school. We'll talk about things. Remember that we are a team here, and you can always ask for help. Okay? Even when we have a student who isn't yet identified, support is still available for both of you." Mr Pawley returned to his office and picked up Max's newly written IEP, which was waiting on his desk for review. He ran his eyes quickly over the list of accommodations for Max, but not much time passed before the bell rang, signalling the end of outdoor recess.

ACCOMMODATIONS
(Accommodations are assumed to be the same for all subjects, unless otherwise indicated)

Instructional Accommodations	Environmental Accommodations	Assessment Accommodations
• provide choices and alternative tasks • chunk information into smaller, more manageable steps • reduce number of expectations for assigned work • teacher proximity when doing whole-class instruction • provide written instructions for tasks	• preferential seating (by the door for easy exit when frustrated) • alternative work environments (quiet area in classroom, study carrel, resource room, hallway) • visual schedule • visual timer	• oral assessment or demonstration when appropriate • reduce number of expectations for assessment • provide word banks and formula cards

Figure 2.2.1 Max's Accommodations
Source: Adapted from Ontario Ministry of Education, 2004. http://www.edu.gov.on.ca/eng/general/elemsec/speced/guide/resource/iepresguid.pdf, p. 53.

Character education Teaching and nurturing the universally positive attributes that provide a standard for behaviour, including academic achievement, respect for diversity, community citizenship, and partnership.

Respect Treating yourself, those around you, and the physical environment with high regard and value. Listening, displaying proper manners, and following the rules are all indications of respect.

Teamwork The sharing of knowledge or skills, working towards a common goal, commitment, and mutual accountability within a group of two or more individuals.

Mr Pawley made sure that he moved over quickly to the bulletin board he was putting up in the hallway, called "Characters with Character!" It was his most recent way to spread the word to students, parents, and staff about their continuing **Character Education** initiative. *This might be a good way to start a conversation about Max's recent behaviour*, he thought.

Max arrived soon after the bell, took his usual pose, back against the wall, head down. He picked up one of the staplers that Mr Pawley had ready to use, and the principal used this as an opportunity to build some behavioural momentum. "Great! It looks like you are ready! As you can see, I already have the background for this bulletin board stapled up, so if you can begin with the edging, that would be helpful. I am going to work on the title."

Max shrugged and began to line up the edging, stapling it into the cork using the heel of his hand. "What is all of this?" A long discussion ensued while Mr Pawley and Max put up the bulletin board. Mr Pawley explained about character education and special words like "**respect**." He went on to tell Max about how he had noticed that many superheroes demonstrated these character traits in books, television, and in movies. He had made colour printouts of the character traits, various superheroes, and how the latter characters demonstrate characteristics like "**teamwork**." Max talked a lot about his favourite superheroes and became very talkative, excited, and animated. He was able to repeat long chunks of dialogue from shows he had watched, while explaining that books "sucked," and that graphic novels were "okay." An idea began to germinate in Mr Pawley's mind while they gathered up scraps of paper and errant staples together, and tossed them into the waiting garbage can and recycling bin. He took a risk.

"Max, you seem to really like these characters, and what they show you that they can do. You said that Superman is really honest, and that Green Lantern gets done what he plans to get done. What about you? Are you like this, too?" asked Mr Pawley, gently, watching Max carefully for a response.

"Um, sometimes. I say what I want to say, but sometimes people—like teachers—get really mad at me and it doesn't work out. But I really want a superpower!"

Mr Pawley smiled, said, "Me, too!" and walked Max back to class, knocking on the classroom door, and making eye contact with Max's teacher, nodding to show that everything was calm. He returned to his desk, picked up Max's IEP draft, and turned towards his **alternative course** in **social skills**.

Special Education Program

To be completed for each subject/course with modified expectations and/or each alternative program with alternative expectations

Student OEN/MIN: *Max*	Subject/Course/Alternative Program: *Social Skills*
Current Level of Achievement: Pre-requisite course _____ N/A _____ Letter grade/Mark _____ N/A _____ Curriculum grade level _____ N/A _____	**Current Level of Achievement for Alternative Program:** *Max has demonstrated inconsistent use of age-appropriate problem-solving strategies when beginning something new or when a challenge is identified. Max has continued to require support in developing and maintaining peer relationships throughout the year as he continues to demonstrate explosive and unpredictable behaviour in the classroom and outside on the playground.*

Annual Program Goal(s): *Max will be able to identify his emotions as frustrated, sad, angry, happy, or relaxed, identify several strategies for coping with each emotion, and implement these strategies with 100% accuracy throughout his day.*

Learning Expectations (List modified/alternative expectations outlining knowledge and/or skills to be assessed, by reporting period. Identify grade level, where appropriate.)	**Teaching Strategies** (List only those that are particular to the student and specific to the learning expectations.)	**Assessment Methods** (Identify the assessment method to be used for each learning expectation.)
Term 1: 1. *Max will be able to identify his emotions as frustrated, sad, angry, happy, or relaxed three times per day with 80% accuracy.*	1. *use social narratives at school and at home to review emotions and strategies.*	• *observations* • *checklists* • *anecdotal notes*
2. *Max will identify 3 strategies for each emotion he is feeling three times per day with 80% accuracy.*	2. *daily check-ins where Max checks in with teacher and identifies his emotion and reviews the corresponding strategies.*	• *observations* • *checklists* • *anecdotal notes*
3. *Max will utilize known strategies when feeling frustrated, sad, angry, happy, or relaxed, three times a day with 50% accuracy and 1–2 teacher prompts.*	3. *provide teacher support including prompting, encouragement, or opportunity for a way out, when Max self-identifies feeling a certain way or when the teacher notices signs of a change in emotional state.*	• *observations* • *anecdotal notes*

Figure 2.2.2 Max's Alternative Course in Social Skills
Source: Adapted from Ontario Ministry of Education, 2004. http://www.edu.gov.on.ca/eng/general/elemsec/speced/guide/resource/iepresguid.pdf, p. 54.

He looked at the objectives, strategies, and assessment tools that the IEP **team** had outlined. *What if,* he thought, *instead of the social narratives—or in addition to them—we use* **Power Cards**? *If we use Power Cards, we can use the motivation of superheroes to help him develop some of these skills.* He pulled out his package of large, lined sticky notes from his desk drawer, took his Power Cards book off his shelf, and sketched out what a Power Card for Max might look like with a question, "How about this for a strategy? I think it would work well for Max."

Just to be sure, he checked the last set of notes from the school's team meeting regarding Max, in particular, that he had crafted into a checklist using one of his computer's organizational apps.

Well, we are getting there, he thought. *This IEP is an excellent step and ensures that the individual programming we have developed for Max can be in place whether or not he is eventually diagnosed. I know we put through a referral to our board's SLP [speech-language pathologist] and* **occupational therapist** *already, but they do have a bit of a waiting list. Our resource teacher is going to start work with Max next week, first by sitting in on his "get to know you" session with the* **child and youth worker**. *Max's parents have already taken care of medical referrals, but I haven't heard from them. It would be really good if we had more assessment information to add to his IEP, but it would also help with our referral to the IPRC.*

STUDENT NEEDS MOVING FORWARD: MAX (GRADE 5)		
Recommendation:	Responsibility of:	✓
Youth worker support recommended for emotional and anxiety issues.	CYW to send consent home	
Encourage parents to access local mental health supports though pediatric doctor assessment/diagnosis.	Principal to discuss with parents	
Learning Resource Teacher (LRT) support—in class and withdrawal.	LRT and Classroom Teacher (CT) to coordinate	
Speech-language, occupational therapy, and psychoeducational assessments recommended.	LRT to submit paperwork	
An IEP will need to be created prior to IPRC to address program accommodations and possible future modifications in all academic areas of language with emphasis on reading/comprehension and Mathematics all at a grade 3 level.	CT in consultation with LRT	
Alternative programming will need to address social anxiety/anxiety/behaviour issues.	CT in consultation with LRT	

Figure 2.2.3 Max's In-School Team Recommendations
Source: Author-generated.

Letting his thoughts develop, he turned back to his computer and logged into his board's email program. He scanned for priorities, and noted with a start that there was indeed an email from Max's parents—quarantined by his spam folder. He moved it to his in-box and clicked on the attachment linked to a brief note: "Please call us to talk about this report." He opened the attachment to have a look and noted that it was part of a university's clinical research. A few comments jumped out immediately. He read:

- Max fits the diagnostic criteria for Neurodevelopmental Disorder associated with Prenatal Alcohol Exposure (under the umbrella of **Fetal Alcohol Spectrum Disorders**—check *DSM-5*).
- Max has significant deficits in visual processing, which are causing learning difficulties in all areas of academic functioning.

Surprised, he sat back in his chair and considered things while he printed out a copy of Max's report. *What does this change? Well, it doesn't change that he needs support in social skills. It does, however, change our academic approach— which is just what the classroom teacher has been telling me—we need to **modify** his core academic subjects like Math and Language based on the recommendations of this report. I had been dragging my heels on this one, because it's such an important decision with potentially long-term consequences for Max. But it also tells me that his school work is clearly an issue, and it has been causing so much of his obvious frustration and behavioural challenges; he has been trying to get out of school work. I think we have a little more work to do before we can finalize this IEP, after all.*

Occupational therapist Regulated professional who works with children to help develop their gross and fine motor muscle development when support is required.

Child and youth worker A support staff member that has been trained to work with children and youth who have social, emotional, or behavioural difficulties.

Fetal Alcohol Spectrum Disorder (FASD) an umbrella term describing the range of effects that can occur in an individual whose mother drank alcohol during pregnancy. These effects include physical, mental, behavioural, and/or learning disabilities with possible lifelong implications.

Modified courses Subjects or courses with changes made to the age-appropriate grade-level expectations to meet a student's learning needs. These changes may involve using expectations developed for a different grade level and/or increasing or decreasing the number and/or complexity of the regular-grade-level curriculum expectations.

A superhero always thinks before he acts in every situation, especially when he is frustrated. He wants you to use his tips for staying cool.

1. Take five deep breaths to help your body relax.
2. Count to 10 in your head.
3. Think about your choices—
   "I can do what I was asked to do"
   "I can ask for help"
   "I can take a break"
4. Make a choice and stick with it.

You can be like a superhero! You can stay cool and make good choices to get the job done!

Figure 2.2.4 Max's Sample Power Card
Sources: InspiredImages/993 images/pixababy.com; wording adapted from Gagnon, 2001.

Mr Pawley made a note to call Max's parents after 4 PM, bundled up his notes and Max's report together with the draft of Max's IEP, and went out to the front area of his school's offices to put them in the resource teacher's mail cubby with an additional comment: "let's talk."

Brief Response Questions

1. Why didn't the first conversation between Max and his teacher work out very well?
2. Is the term a "bad day" the best one the principal could have used? Why or why not?
3. Why did Max's teacher and principal ignore Max throwing a scrap of paper onto the floor?
4. Explain why Max's teacher thinks that a new diagnosis really doesn't change much of anything. Do you agree or disagree? Why?
5. Are IEPs ever finalized? Explain.
6. Is the hallway an appropriate location for this kind of conversation and/or support? Why or why not?
7. In what ways do you think the resource teacher is already supporting this situation?
8. Explain "behavioural momentum" and how it might help Max. Be sure to use a source from the field of Applied Behaviour Analysis.

In-Depth Response Questions

1. Choose one of Max's learning expectations and compare it to each element of a SMART goal and explain the process of planning the goal. Following is an example of SMART goal setting for students:
   https://www.scholastic.com/teachers/blog-posts/genia-connell/setting-almost-smart-goals-my-students/
   Analyze your comparison, make a conclusion, and recommend any change(s).
2. Create a Power Card for Max, describing its components with detail.
3. What did Mr Pawley mean by the statement that modifying courses is an "important decision with potentially long-term consequences"? Explain in detail, or disagree and support your disagreement.
4. What accommodations would you consider adding to Max's IEP due to his "significant deficits in visual processing"? List and explain each one in detail, providing relevant quotes from academic sources, professional sources, and Ministry sources, as well as case study details.

Case 3: Cassalena's Pathway

Teachers were already well into preparations for September—moving around furniture, setting up welcoming bulletin boards, arranging services for their students—all in anticipation of the students' arrival. This latter action was especially true for Cassalena's teacher, Ms Ikeda. So far this week, Ms Ikeda had phoned Cassalena's parents to check in with them, met with the behaviour consultant that had been working with Cassalena and her parents throughout the summer weeks when Cassalena attended local day camps, and was in the process of emailing the occupational therapist who had done a consult as a result of a board referral back in January. Though the assessment had been completed in June, Ms Ikeda had just received the full report—and she had a few questions. *It feels great to sit down,* Ms Ikeda thought, pushing her damp bangs off her face. *I always forget how hot it still is at this time of year, especially inside the walls of St Paul Catholic School.* As she typed, she thought back to the behavioural consultation during the last school year as a result of Cassalena's almost constant engagement in problem behaviours such as hand-flapping that were interfering with her ability to complete her academic tasks.

"Sensory, sensory, sensory," the behaviour consultant had emphasized. "I have completed a functional behaviour assessment of Cassalena—as requested—including observation using an ABC form and a scatterplot, as well as two different indirect measures of behavioural functioning. Perhaps you remember? All of you completed the MAS and the FAST, and rated questions like, "Would the behavior occur continuously, over and over, if this were left alone for long periods of time (for example, several hours)?" (Durand & Crimmings, 1992). All of my analysis is written up in my report, but it's essential for all of us to understand—even you, Ms Ikeda, since you will have Cassalena next year in Grade 6—that the function of this behaviour appears to be strongly sensory oriented."

	Sensory	Escape	Attention	Tangible
	6	2	1	3
	4	0	1	3
	5	4	2	2
	4	2	2	4
Total Score =	19	8	6	12
Mean Score = (divide total score by 4)	4.75	2.0	1.5	3.0
Relative Ranking = (high score to low score)	1	3	4	2

Figure 2.3.1 Cassalena's MAS Analysis
Source: Adapted from Durand & Crimmings, 1992.

Ms Ikeda rested her chin on the palm of her hand and remembered further.
"So," the behaviour consultant had continued, "what we want to do next, since it's really important for Cassalena to be able to focus on her academic goals, is

Antecedent-Behaviour-Consequence (ABC) form (or chart) An assessment tool to examine the frequency and causes of certain undesirable behaviours. The form includes three columns to record the antecedent (what happened just before the behaviour, or the "trigger"), the undesirable behaviour, and the consequence.

Scatterplot A type of plot, graph, or diagram used to display patterns of behaviour over time.

Motivation Assessment Scale (MAS) An assessment that measures problem behaviours in individuals with developmental disabilities with the goal of finding appropriate replacement behaviours.

The Functional Analysis Screening Tool (FAST) A questionnaire on the relationship or correlation between problematic behaviours and any antecedent and consequence events.

Operationalize
To express or define something, usually the cause of a behaviour, in relation to a series of assessments or trials that determine or prove the cause of the behaviour.

to find a way to replace this sensory-oriented flapping behaviour, which we had defined, or **operationalized** (so far), as flapping her hands up and down from the wrist at least two times in a row in quick succession (not in order to cool herself down or to wave away insects).

"We want to find a way for Cassalena to get her sensory needs met and be able to focus on the curriculum, too. I suggest we complete a 'competing behaviours pathway' (O'Neill, Albin, Storey, Horner, & Sprague, 2014). But first, I think that we should refer Cassalena for an OT assessment to make sure we are going to use the right sensory tools to meet her needs. We want to do this right, especially given Cassalena's complex set of past diagnoses indicated on her IEP."

ASSESSMENT DATA

List relevant educational, medical/health (hearing, vision, physical, neurological), psychological, speech/language, occupational, physiotherapy, and behavioural assessments.

Information Source	Date	Summary of Results
Speech/Language Assessment	Grade 2	Notable difficulty with spatial and qualitative concepts; receptive language is age appropriate. Expressive language skills delayed. Remediation on semantic skills is required. Has difficulty with naming labels, repetition of phrases and sentences.
Audiological Report	Grade 2	Normal hearing and middle-ear function in both ears. When competing speech was presented to both ears, a slight deficiency found in speech perception.
Medical Report	Grade 4	Diagnosis of Autism Spectrum Disorder

Figure 2.3.2 Cassalena's Assessment List

Source: Adapted from Ontario Ministry of Education, 2004. http://www.edu.gov.on.ca/eng/general/elemsec/speced/guide/resource/iepresguid.pdf, p.52.

This OT report was what Ms Ikeda was unfolding, following a referral, a wait, and then the summertime. She read through the background—nothing surprising. She read through the assessment procedures—nothing new. Then she jumped to what she felt was highly important for Cassalena's functioning in her inclusive classroom: the recommendations, which appeared in a list of bulleted points, close to the end of this formal report.

Well, she considered. *There is a lot we can do with this. I think the only piece that won't work is the idea of bringing in others to scribe and this idea of "ongoing" EA support. While I do have an EA in my classroom for at least two periods a day, the EA supports a number of students and is assigned to our classroom—she is not "sitting beside" specific students. Sometimes, she spends time circulating among all the students so I can have more time with my students who need more individualized supports. And going back to the scribe idea, we already do that for Cassalena, but it is pretty time consuming. In fact, I was thinking of starting to use some speech-to-text tools like Dragon NaturallySpeaking. This would help her to be more independent and more efficient, and get ready for the demands of high school.*

Occupational Therapy Visit Report	Lynne Mann, OT
	Cassalena Grade 5

Assessment and Recommendations

- Cassalena's visual–motor integration skills are below her age level. This will continue to affect the formation of printed letters and written ideas.
- Cassalena appears to lack strength and coordination when holding a pencil.
- When Cassalena becomes anxious or excited, hand-flapping behaviour is observed. Accommodations will be necessary.
- A scribe is recommended in the classroom to assist. A peer tutor is preferable.
- Cassalena can be impulsive and very emotional, at times demonstrating off-task behaviour. Regular physical breaks will be necessary from desk work to help Cassalena manage her energy.
- Ongoing supervision by an adult—possibly an educational assistant—is required to support work habits and fine motor output.
- Use of a pediatric weighted therapy belt will help Cassalena with self-calming, balance, and increased body awareness.
- Use of a "stress ball" will improve Cassalena's focus, help her absorb more information, self-regulate, and provide a calming influence. This will help get her hands and fingers moving in coordination.

Figure 2.3.3 Cassalena's OT Recommendations
Source: Author-generated.

After making some notes—a welcome break from setting up her desks—Ms Ikeda went down the hallway to consult with the resource teacher, who was no doubt immersed in updating IEPs already, and to place the OT report in Cassalena's OSR. Then she remembered the list of in-school team recommendations that they had also created for Cassalena near year-end last year, so they could be ready to go during her grade six year, which is—of course—just beginning. Thankful for all the hard work that the in-school team had put into this proactive planning, she turned around, went back to the computer, and pulled up her notes to compare.

In-School Team Meeting Notes June: Cassalena Grade 6 in September

When program planning, REMEMBER:
1. Educational assistant at arm's length; ongoing buddy–peer grouping to increase social skills.
2. Continue speech-language therapy with updates.
3. Follow up with OT recommendations and behavioural assessments.
4. Continued focus on communication and social skills.
5. Arrange a new community assessment to assist with IEP transition planning.
6. Remind family to arrange an annual pediatric physical examination.
7. IEP Development Focus: Alternative Programming—communication and social behaviour; Modified Programming—Reading, Writing, and Math (all two grade levels below).
8. Incorporate movement and music into physical activity breaks.

Figure 2.3.4 Ms Ikeda's Notes from June's In-School Team Meeting
Source: Author-generated.

Relaxation station
Also known as a calming corner or quiet corner, a relaxation station is an area in the classroom designed to provide a space for all students to access when they need a short break, quiet time to think through something they are frustrated with, or to regroup. The relaxation station contains comfortable areas to sit, may include sensory-based activities designed to provide a calming effect, and is an inclusive way to provide students the opportunity to de-escalate within the classroom.

Evidence-based practices Teaching practices that are evaluated as effective based on data gathered over time demonstrating their effectiveness.

She spoke aloud, "Yup, there are definitely some commonalities here for next steps that can be written into her new IEP for the fall term." *Time to check back in with the resource teacher and the parent, and to connect with the behaviour therapist again. It's a good thing we already had that going. It sounds like the best next step for classroom set-up, then, might be to craft a **relaxation station** for Cassalena to use, as well as all my other students. I was reading about them just the other day and I think it can work for us as a great place for a mental break, using those stress balls suggested by the OT, and lots of other de-stressing ideas and tools. I read an article related to self-regulation with some examples in it just the other day.*

Ms Ikeda pulled up the article in *Education Canada* and read:

While some students continue to struggle in areas such as everyday transitions, they learn coping skills, such as taking the initiative to move over to the table named "Australia" (after *Alexander and the Terrible, Horrible, No Good, Very Bad Day* [by Judith Viorst]) for a break. As Labatt describes it, self-regulation skills "bleed into everything else" that happens in the classroom—and in life beyond it." (Bonnett & Maich, 2014)

I think this is my very next step for today, Ms Ikeda decided, and went off to accomplish this task—and many more—to set up September for success.

Brief Response Questions

1. Read http://www.cea-ace.ca/education-canada/article/foundational-%E2%80%9Cr%E2%80%9D (The Foundational "R") and describe one idea or strategy that you have used—or would use—in a classroom.
2. Have you ever taught social skills—or would you? If yes, how? If no, why not?
3. What is your opinion of this model of EA support?
4. What is one benefit, and one detriment, of scribing for students?
5. How might Cassalena's hand-flapping interfere with her academic success at school?
6. What is Dragon NaturallySpeaking?

In-Depth Response Questions

1. Find a recent, peer-reviewed research summary on "buddy" skills (e.g., peer-mediated social skills) and summarize it in 3–5 paragraphs.
2. Are sensory interventions considered to be **evidence-based practices**? Discuss. Support your discussion with at least two academic sources.

continued

3. Explore Google's assistive technology options (https://www.google.ca/accessibility/products-features.html) and comment on at least three.
4. Explain the process of modifying a core academic subject like Math, describing at least two of these steps in detail.
5. Research the connection between physical activity and challenging behaviour. What did you find? Summarize your explorations in at least three paragraphs.
6. What would Cassalena's student profile look like? Please use the template provided:

STUDENT PROFILE

Name: _____ Gender: _____ Date of Birth: _____

School: _____

Student OEN/MIN: _____ Principal: _____

Current Grade/Special Class: _____ School Year: _____

Most Recent IPRC Date: _____ Date Annual Review Waived by Parent/Guardian: _____

Exceptionality: _____

IPRC Placement Decision (*check one*)

☐ Regular class with indirect support   ☐ Special education class with partial integration
☐ Regular class with resource assistance   ☐ Special education class full-time
☐ Regular class with withdrawal assistance

Figure 2.3.5 Student Profile

Source: Adapted from Ontario Ministry of Education, 2004. http://www.edu.gov.on.ca/eng/general/elemsec/speced/guide/resource/iepresguid.pdf, p.52.

Case 4: Vanessa's Bully

Guest Contributor: Grace Maich, MA Student
(Critical Sociology), Brock University

At dinner one night Vanessa's mother, Priya, noticed she was not eating. "Is everything okay, Vanessa?" she asked, concerned about her daughter. Ever since starting school last month, Vanessa had been acting differently than her usual cheery self. Vanessa and her twin sister Christina had been separated into different grade four classrooms, and were apart for the first time in their schooling career. Christina liked to be in the same class as Vanessa because Vanessa had **Down Syndrome** and some trouble making friends because of what others seemed to think was an unusual appearance and because speech difficulties made it easier for her to communicate using sign language. Still, she had always been a friendly girl and brought lots of kids to her birthday parties, so her parents had limited concerns about her being in a class without her sister. However, her tantrums, which were normally rare occurrences, had started happening nearly every day. Her previously big appetite had also disappeared.

Vanessa signed that she didn't want to eat because the food tasted bad, shoved her plate away, and ran to hide in her room. Christina also started fiddling with the food on her plate, pushing it around with her fork. "Christina," Priya said quietly, "is something going on at school that you're not telling us about?"

Christina frowned. "The girls in Vanessa's class are so mean. A girl named Jasmine and her friends pretend to be nice to her during class, but they make fun of her when we're trying to play during recess. Sometimes they pretend to help her with her classwork, but they really tell her the wrong answers!"

"I was wondering about that." Priya shook her head. "She brought home a spelling test yesterday and she got everything wrong. Spelling isn't her best subject but she works hard and usually does okay."

Vanessa's father, Adrian, stood up abruptly. "I'm going to go talk to her." He went to her room and sat down on the edge of the bed where Vanessa had stubbornly covered herself in pillows. "Can you come out and talk to me for a moment?"

Vanessa tried to shake her head, but that only dislodged the pillows and gave her father a chance to speak. "I hear some girls in your class are **bullying** you. Is this true?"

Vanessa shrugged. "They're nice," she signed, "but sometimes they tell me things that are wrong. Then they say sorry because they were confused."

"Does Mr Vega know about this?" Adrian asked, growing concerned at how long this could have been going on at school. Juan Vega was Vanessa's teacher this year, and he'd always told her parents he would be happy to accommodate Vanessa, however he could, but also wanted to try to include her in the regular classwork. Adrian wondered if it were possible he was trying too hard to make her fit in.

"He told me not to talk to them during class, but they always talk to me," Vanessa responded. "He moved my seat so I'm not sitting near Jasmine, but her friends talk to me too."

Vanessa's father helped her up to bring her back to the dinner table. "I know you're scared and upset about this situation, but we're going to fix it, okay?" He

Down Syndrome A naturally occurring chromosomal arrangement in which additional genetic material attaches to chromosome 21 during early cell division. Characteristics vary greatly but include mild to severe physical and learning implications.

Bullying Aggressive behaviour meant to cause harm, fear, or distress that is typically repeated over time. Bullying occurs in a situation where there is a real or perceived power imbalance.

placed her back in her seat and moved her food plate back toward her in case she wanted to eat. "I think we need to talk about some of Vanessa's options. Do you think the teachers would agree to transfer Vanessa into Christina's class? It's still near the beginning of the year, so it shouldn't disrupt too much."

At the suggestion, Vanessa began shaking her head quickly. "I like my teacher. He's nice and understands me," she signed.

Her parents looked at each other and Adrian raised his eyebrows. They wanted their daughter to be able to do her best in class, but they didn't want to distress her further by moving classrooms and having her adjust to a new teacher and classmates. "I guess Vanessa and Christina are going to have to learn to live independently from one another sooner or later," Priya said. "I think it's time we set up a meeting with Mr Vega to figure out our options."

Mr Vega was happy to arrange a meeting for the following evening. He agreed that Vanessa's situation needed to be addressed, but wasn't entirely sure how to deal with it appropriately. He also suggested Vanessa and Christina both attend the meeting to get their input, as Christina knew Vanessa almost better than anybody. The family showed up at his classroom the next evening, and Priya was particularly upset about an incident that had happened earlier. "I'm sure you know this, Juan, but today at recess another girl from your class joined my daughters to play. When they got home, they told me the girl was following Vanessa around and imitating her **sign language** use, and continued to do so when they got into class."

"Yes," Mr Vega said with a frown, "the girl's name is Jasmine and she's been a particular problem for Vanessa since class started. I've asked her to leave her alone several times and I've moved her desk to a different part of the classroom. At this point, she is leaving Vanessa alone during class, but Jasmine's friends still bother her. Jasmine's been in trouble a few times and it doesn't seem to have any effect on her, and neither have the notes I sent home to her parents. I want to do anything I can to help Vanessa. Has she considered changing classes to be with her sister?"

Vanessa shook her head and hid her face in her hands. Christina spoke up. "She's used to the classroom and she wouldn't be safe at recess anyway."

Adrian smiled at his daughter and ruffled her hair. "We certainly don't want to cause any major upheaval for Vanessa if it might not solve the problem."

Mr Vega nodded his agreement and shuffled around some papers on his desk, unsure about how to proceed. "Well, I have seen an idea in some schools that might help you out a bit. It's a little less official, but have you heard of **restorative justice**?"

Both parents shook their heads. "It's a fairly new practice, but it is certainly gaining popularity. Basically, we would hold a meeting or a series of meetings with all of you along with Jasmine and her parents. If Vanessa has a social worker or other caregiver we could invite that person along as well. Vanessa can share her problems and we'll work together to find an appropriate solution. This gives Jasmine an opportunity to really understand how she's affecting all of you."

The parents exchanged glances. "I'm not so sure about this. You mentioned Jasmine's parents wouldn't respond to notes you sent home. I doubt they care enough to attend a meeting about their child's behaviour," Priya pointed out.

"Perhaps not," Mr Vega said, "but there's only one way to find out. Remember, the point of all this is to make Vanessa's school experience easier. If we have to

Sign language
A system of visually perceived language that uses hand gestures, their placement relative to the body, as well as facial expressions and other body movements to communicate meaning.

Restorative justice
An approach to dealing with conflicts, with a focus on repairing the harm done to individuals and the community rather than on punishing the offender. The overall goal is to develop strategies to move forward without the offender repeating the same offences.

Figure 2.4.1 Restorative Justice Typology
Source: Wachtel, T., 2012. Defining restorative. *International Institute for Restorative Practices*, p. 2.

find a different way of going about this, we will. For now, how do you feel about the idea?"

Adrian glanced at his daughters. "Vanessa, we have an idea about something that could help you." Vanessa and Christina, who up to this point had been whispering and giggling to each other, looked up. Adrian continued. "How do you feel about having a meeting with Jasmine and her parents? We'll talk to them about the bullying and come to a solution together. After all, bullying is hard not only for you, but can be hard on the bully, too."

Vanessa shook her head once again and signed that it was scary to talk to her bully. Mr Vega walked over to her and knelt down beside her chair. "I know you're scared, but you're a very brave girl. It was brave of you to come to this meeting at all, okay? We won't make you say anything you don't want to. If this doesn't work, we'll figure out something else."

To her parents' surprise, Vanessa reached out and gave her teacher a hug. "Thank you," she signed. "I will do it."

Mr Vega stood up and looked at Vanessa's parents. "I'll send you an email once I've contacted Jasmine's parents and let you know what we can work out."

Vanessa's parents shook hands with him. "Thank you for working with us. I don't want to single out any of your students but Vanessa's been having a really hard time this year."

"It's no problem at all," Mr Vega said. "After all, it's my job to help students learn, and neither of them are going to learn well in a situation like this. I'll see you sometime next week."

When the family arrived at home, they sat down to eat dinner. For the first time in days, Vanessa ate her whole meal without complaining.

Brief Response Questions

1. Would Vanessa have an IEP? Why or why not?
2. List three to five signs of Down Syndrome that teachers might recognize in the classroom environment.
3. It appears that Vanessa has some verbal language. Why would she use sign language as well?
4. Do you think that having a sibling in a school could help or hurt this bullying situation? Why?
5. What does "integrate her into the regular classwork" mean? Would you have explained this differently? If yes, how? If not, why not?
6. What negative effects can bullying have on a bully (i.e., bully victims)? Use "What's a Bully Victim?" (Marini, Dane, & Volk, 2010) to help frame your response: http://www.education.com/reference/article/what-is-a-bully-victim/

In-Depth Response Questions

1. Do you think or feel that transitions are particularly challenging for Vanessa? Why or why not? Describe three to five actions that you would include in the transition-plan component of Vanessa's IEP.
2. What is Vanessa's first language? Explain in detail.
3(a). List at least four of Vanessa's courses, and check off either modified, accommodated, or alternative. Then, explain why you would make each of these decisions.

SUBJECTS, COURSES, OR ALTERNATIVE PROGRAMS TO WHICH THE IEP APPLIES

Identify each as Modified (MOD), Accommodated only (AC), or Alternative (ALT)

1. _____ ☐ MOD ☐ AC ☐ ALT	6. _____ ☐ MOD ☐ AC ☐ ALT
2. _____ ☐ MOD ☐ AC ☐ ALT	7. _____ ☐ MOD ☐ AC ☐ ALT
3. _____ ☐ MOD ☐ AC ☐ ALT	8. _____ ☐ MOD ☐ AC ☐ ALT
4. _____ ☐ MOD ☐ AC ☐ ALT	9. _____ ☐ MOD ☐ AC ☐ ALT
5. _____ ☐ MOD ☐ AC ☐ ALT	10. _____ ☐ MOD ☐ AC ☐ ALT

Figure 2.4.2 Subjects, Courses, or Alternative Programs

Source: Ontario Ministry of Education, 2004. http://www.edu.gov.on.ca/eng/general/elemsec/speced/guide/resource/iepresguid.pdf, p. 53. © Queen's Printer for Ontario, 2004. Reproduced with permission.

continued

3(b). If you noted any modified courses for Vanessa, complete the below special education program form for one of these courses for one term. Then, discuss any long-term implications of modified academic courses.

Special Education Program

To be completed for each subject/course with modified expectations and/or each alternative program with alternative expectations.

Student OEN/MIN:	Subject/Course/Alternative Program:

Current Level of Achievement: Pre-requisite course _____ Letter Grade/Mark _____ Curriculum Grade Level _____	Current Level of Achievement for Alternative Program:

Annual Program Goal(s): A goal statement describing what the student can reasonably be expected to accomplish by the end of the school year in a particular subject, course, or alternative program.

Learning Expectations	Teaching Strategies	Assessment Methods
(List modified/alternative expectations outlining knowledge and/or skills to be assessed, by reporting period. Identify grade level, where appropriate.)	(List only those that are particular to the student and specific to the learning expectations.)	(Identify the assessment method to be used for each learning expectation.)

Figure 2.4.3 Modified Program Template
Source: Adapted from Ontario Ministry of Education, 2004. http://www.edu.gov.on.ca/eng/general/elemsec/speced/guide/resource/iepresguid.pdf, p. 54.

3(c). If you noted any alternative courses for Vanessa, complete the below special education program form for one of these courses for one term.

Special Education Program

To be completed for each subject/course with modified expectations and/or each alternative program with alternative expectations.

Student OEN/MIN:	Subject/Course/Alternative Program:

Current Level of Achievement: Pre-requisite course _____ Letter Grade/Mark _____ Curriculum Grade Level _____	Current Level of Achievement for Alternative Program:

Annual Program Goal(s): A goal statement describing what the student can reasonably be expected to accomplish by the end of the school year in a particular subject, course, or alternative program.

Learning Expectations	Teaching Strategies	Assessment Methods
(List modified/alternative expectations outlining knowledge and/or skills to be assessed, by reporting period. Identify grade level, where appropriate.)	(List only those that are particular to the student and specific to the learning expectations.)	(Identify the assessment method to be used for each learning expectation.)

Figure 2.4.4 Modified Program Template
Source: Adapted from Ontario Ministry of Education, 2004. http://www.edu.gov.on.ca/eng/general/elemsec/speced/guide/resource/iepresguid.pdf, p. 54.

4. Summarize the practice of restorative justice when it comes to bullying in schools, referring to "Improving School Climate to Reduce Bullying" (Smith, n.d.) found at http://www.cea-ace.ca/education-canada/article/improving-school-climate-reduce-bullying

Case 5: Ms Ikeda's Relaxation Station

Cardboard cubbies
Created with a trifold cardboard divider, these privacy screens can be used as a study carrel placed on top of a desk.

Well, that took a lot more time than I thought, reflected Ms Ikeda, looking at her weekend's work. *It's a good thing I brought some helpers.* She smiled at her two daughters, who had wanted to come in with her on the weekend to help set up her classroom—with promises of pizza and movie coupons afterward. They were currently sharing a set of noise-cancelling headphones, impressing each other with how well it blocked out sound by testing out their various hand-held devices. *And just in time!* She stepped back from her grade six/seven classroom corner, now labelled the "Relaxation Station," and looked at it with a sense of pleasure and accomplishment . . . as well as exhaustion. *I think it's going to be worth it, though.* She turned around when she heard a polite knock on her open door, and saw her colleague and friend walking towards her with a huge smile.

Time-out Following the occurrence of a problem behaviour, a student is given a time-out from attention to that problem behaviour, such as the activity, space, or peers who reinforced the problem behaviour. The goal is to prevent future displays of the problem behaviour.

After catching up with summer events, her friend inquired, "So what's all this?"

"Oh," responded Ms Ikeda, eager to show off her new domain, "this is our class's new zone. One of my students has a recommendation for a cool-off spot in the classroom, and I thought it would make sense for everyone to use it. There is kind of nowhere to take a break right in my classroom, and it's really hard to manage having to send students to other rooms and teachers for a bit of a change of pace or a quiet spot. Our use of the resource room will probably be cut in half!" She smiled, and walked over to her new set-up. "You can see that I have placed two of these shorter bookcases together to make a semi-private spot here in the corner. I actually found them in our storage space with a sign that said, 'TAKE ME' on it. They are a bit battered, but perfect for our purposes. So, I have left space for students to enter and exit, but the two walls and the two bookcases make a nice, cozy spot, which I can still monitor easily from most places in the classroom. I put one of our extra desk/chair combo units in here, and then I picked up one of those three-sided **cardboard cubbies** and put it on top. Remember those ones we used to study in at the university library? Kind of like that, but just a little cardboard version."

Five-point scale
A visual system that can help to organize the thought process of an individual when confronted with difficult moments, particularly those that require social understanding or emotional regulation. Breaking a previously determined problem area into five visually illustrated parts can support students during communication breakdown, and help them make sense of the reactions and feelings of themselves or others.

"I get it," said the grade seven teacher. "So this gives students who need a quiet study space a little bit of visual separation between them and the rest of the class."

"Right!" responded Ms Ikeda. "That's it. And then—as you can see—we have a few sets of noise-cancelling headphones if they need a break from sound as well as sight. Then, beside the desk, I have brought in some soft seating . . . it's kind of like what I saw in our kindergarten class's cozy corner. But I thought—why should only kindergarten get this great stuff? My students can use it, too! So, I have this big, soft chair where students can actually curl up—if they want to do so."

"So you use it like a **time-out**?"

Break card A tool that provides a student with the option to ask for a break when feeling frustrated. A break card can be a very simple card with the word "break" on it or a picture of a quiet area. The student or the teacher can use the break card to request or suggest a break if it seems that one is needed.

"Nooooo, definitely not. It's really different—the whole point is for STUDENTS to start to understand when they themselves need a break—to work on developing their self-regulation skills. At first, I will help them to know when is a good time to take a break, and I will put that strategy on our class's **five-point scale**. It's not quite ready yet. Then, I will show them how to use this **break card** to request a break. The deal is, though, that they have to use the visual timer to count down the time in the relaxation station—they can't stay forever. I am also working on setting up a set of lessons around the Zones of Regulation. It's a great program that actually teaches techniques around relaxation strategies like 'Lazy 8 Breathing.' As soon as we go through these lessons, I am going to post visuals reminding students how to use the strategies, and I am going to keep samples right in the relaxation station, posted on this wall." She pointed to a sticky note on the wall as her reminder to add these pieces later. "I saw tons of great ideas on Instagram and then I thought I would order the book for myself. I suspect it will get a ton of use! Come on in . . . and let's look at the shelves. I am pretty excited about what I have put together. Check it out!"

Ms Ikeda's friend stepped in and started picking up items on the shelves. "I recognize these!" She squeezed a few sizes and shapes of **stress balls**, and pulled and stretched some other oddly shaped items. "Great! I have one of these beside my computer at home for when my technology is misbehaving . . . but what's this?" She picked up a large plastic jar with a lid tightly attached. "It looks like the lid is glued on."

"Shake it! I found it on Pinterest by searching for 'calm down corner.' It has all different names but I like '**hush bottle**.' It has glitter in it that moves and settles. It's pretty soothing to watch! I actually found the instructions on a parenting blog. Then I have some picture books—those kind that are specifically about social-emotional–behavioural topics, as well as a few that just happen to have stories about students who have difficulty self-regulating. Then, I am going to have each student bring in some of their favourite things that they find calming. I have a bin set up for each of them. I was thinking maybe they would like to bring in family pictures, or a

Stress balls Small, malleable toys in the shape of a ball designed to fit in the hand and provide sensory relief by squeezing.

Hush bottle One term for a sensory bottle; a clear bottle filled with liquid and glitter and then sealed. It can be used to help calm a frustrated or upset student.

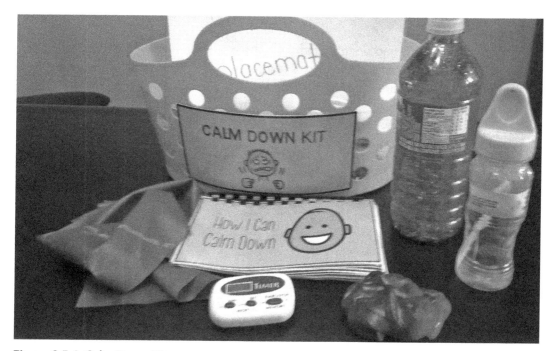

Figure 2.5.1 Calm Down Kit
Source: Monique Somma (used with permission).

photo of their pets, or something like that. I also have these sheets," she noted, pulling them out of a bin, "where students can reflect on their self-regulation strategies."

They stepped outside again. "Right before you go in," Ms Ikeda pointed out, "I have posted instructions that I adapted from 'Teachers Pay Teachers' providing a visual reminder of how to use this space."

"What do you think?"

The Relaxation Station

So, you are feeling a little upset
(or maybe REALLY upset! And that's OK!)
You made a GREAT choice by finding this corner!
Here's what you can do:

1. GET COMFY
   - use the beanbag chair
   - relax on the carpet
   - stand
   - whatever feels comfortable for you

2. BREATHE
   - Breathe in slowly and deeply. Find the bottom of your lungs and fill them up with air all the way to the top. Hold for a few seconds, then exhale all of the air out and start over again. Take 5 deep breaths.

3. FIND A STRESS RELIEVER
   - use a stress ball or glitter bottle
   - draw a picture
   - listen to music
   - build something
   - whatever works for you

4. TAKE TWO
   - take 2 minutes to calm down. If you are still upset after 2 minutes, we can talk about it.

REMEMBER: This space is a safe place for you to calm down and take time for yourself—respect it!

Figure 2.5.2 The Relaxation Station
Source: Author-generated.

Brief Response Questions

1. Browse through online examples of relaxation stations. What other names can you find for this type of environmental strategy for self-regulation (e.g., cozy corner)?
2. Why would a stress ball be placed in a relaxation station?
3. What process(es) would you put in place for entry into the relaxation station?
4. What process(es) would you put in place for exit from the relaxation station?
5. Find and describe an example of a picture book related to self-regulation or another social–emotional–behavioural topic that you might include in a relaxation station.

In-Depth Response Questions

1. Name, describe, and explain two other elements you would add to Ms Ikeda's relaxation station. Rationalize your choices with support from peer-reviewed literature.
2. Name, describe, and explain one or two elements you would remove from Ms Ikeda's relaxation station. Support your choices.
3. How would you introduce Cassalena—or another student—to the relaxation station and teach that child how to use it? Explain these processes in detail.
4. How would you develop a relaxation-type station for an intermediate-aged classroom? What would it look like? Explain your elements with detail.
5. Do you think that every classroom should have some type of cool-down space? Support your answer with literature and/or anecdotes.

Suggested Resources

AD/HD & FASD
https://www.ncbi.nlm.nih.gov/pmc/articles/PMC2938300/

Behavioural Momentum
https://www.youtube.com/watch?v=8irK0qU5OgI

Calm Down Corner
https://www.pinterest.com/explore/calm-down-corner/

Canada FASD Research Network
https://canfasd.ca/

Canada's Self-Esteem Project: Teasing & Bullying
http://selfesteem.dove.ca/en/Articles/Written/Teasing_and_bullying.aspx?gclid
    =CNSE0si-l9ECFduPswodimoHHA&gclsrc=aw.ds

Canadian Down Syndrome Society
http://www.cdss.ca

Current Research Regarding Time-out
http://aie.apsea.ca/assets/files/info-papers/current-research-time-outv02.pdf

Developmental Coordination Disorder
https://canchild.ca/en/diagnoses/developmental-coordination-disorderDove

Dragon NaturallySpeaking
http://www.nuance.com/dragon/index.htm

FASD Fact Sheet
https://canfasd.ca/media/fasd-fact-sheet/

FASD National Screening Tool Kit
http://www.caphc.org/fasd/fasd-national-screening-tool-kit/

(The) Incredible 5-Point Scale
http://www.5pointscale.com/

Power Cards
https://www.erinoakkids.ca/ErinoakKids/media/EOK_Documents/Autism_Resources/
Power-Cards.pdf

References

Abarca, J., Bedard, A., Carlson, D., Carlson, L., Hertzberg, J., Louie, B., . . .
Sullivan, J. (2000). *Introductory engineering design:
A projects-based approach* (3rd ed.). https://itll.colorado.edu/images/uploads/
courses_workshops/geen1400/textbook/cover.pdf

Autism in Education (2016). *Information paper: Research to inform practice: Current
research regarding time-out.* http://aie.apsea.ca/assets/files/info-papers/current-
research-time-outv02.pdf

Barbetta, P.M., Norona, K.L., & Bicard, D.F. (2005). Classroom behavior management:
A dozen common mistakes and what to do instead. *Preventing School Failure, 49*(3),
11–19.

Bonnett, T., & Maich, K. (2014, January). The foundational "R." *Education
Canada, 54*(1). http://www.cea-ace.ca/education-canada/article/
foundational-%E2%80%9Cr%E2%80%9D

Buron, K.D. (2006). *The incredible 5-point scale.* Autism Asperger Publishing Co.
http://www.5pointscale.com/5-point_scale_paper.pdf

Canadian Down Syndrome Society. (2009). *Types of Down syndrome.* http://www.cdss.ca
/information/general-information/types-of-downsyndrome.html

CanChild. (2016). *Developmental coordination disorder.* https://canchild.ca/en/diagnoses
/developmental-coordination-disorder

Durand, V.M., & Crimmings, D.B. (1992). *Motivation Assessment Scale: Administration
guide.* Monaco & Associates Incorporated.

Gagnon, E. (2001). *Power cards: Using special interests to motivate children and youth with
Asperger syndrome and autism.* AAPC Publishing.

Gresham, F., & Elliott, S. (1987). The relationship between adaptive behaviour and social
skills: Issues in definition and assessment. *Journal of Special Education, 21,* 167–81.

Iwata, G., DeLeon, I.G., & Roscoe, E.M. (2013). Reliability and validity of the Functional Analysis Screening Tool. *Journal of Applied Behavior Analysis 46*(1), 271–84. doi:10.1002/jaba.31

Marini, Z., Dane, A., & Volk, T. (2010). *What's a bully-victim?* http://www.education.com/reference/article/what-is-a-bully-victim/

Olweus, D. (1993). *Bullying at school: What we know and what we can do*. Malden, MA: Blackwell Publishing.

O'Neill, R.E., Albin, R.W., Storey, K., Horner, R.H., & Sprague, J.R. (2014). *Functional assessment and program development for problem behavior: A practical handbook* (3rd ed.). Stamford, CT: Cengage.

Ontario Ministry of Education. (2001). *Special education: A guide for educators*. http://www.tncdsb.on.ca/new/resources/SPED%20A%20Guide%20for%20Educators%2001.pdf

Ontario Ministry of Education. (2004). *The individual education plan: A resourceguide*. Toronto, ON: Queen's Printer for Ontario. http://www.edu.gov.on.ca/eng/general/elemsec/speced/guide/resource/ipresguid.pdf

Ontario Ministry of Education. (2008). *Finding common ground: Character development in Ontario schools, K–12*. http://ddsb.ca/Students/SafeSchools/Documents/Finding_Common_Ground.pdf

Ontario Ministry of Education. (2013). *Bullying, we can all help stop it: A guide for parents of elementary and secondary school students*. https://edu.gov.on.ca/eng/multi/english/BullyingEN.pdf

Niagara Catholic District School Board. (2004). *Transition planning for the individual education plan*. http://www.edugains.ca/resourcesSpecEd/IEP&Transitions/BoardDevelopedResources/TransitionPlanniTr/Samples/TransitionPlanfortheIndividualEducationPlan(IEP)_Sample_NCDSB.pdf

Peel District School Board. (2016). *Character attributes*. http://www.peelschools.org/aboutus/safeschools/characterattributes/Pages/default.aspx

Ray-Subramanian, C. (2013). Motivation Assessment Scale. In F.R. Volkmar (Ed.)., *Encyclopedia of autism spectrum disorders* (1918–20). New York, NY: Springer-Verlag. doi:10.1007/978-1-4419-1698-3_1680

Smith, D. (n.d.). Improving school climate to reduce bullying. *Education Canada*. http://www.cea-ace.ca/education-canada/article/improving-school-climate-reduce-bullying

Wachtel, T. (2012). Defining restorative. *International Institute for Restorative Practices*, 1–12.

Williams, J.F., & Smith, V.C. (2015). Fetal alcohol spectrum disorders. *Pediatrics, 136*(5), e1395–e406.

Intermediate 3

Introduction

Chapter 3 is set around intermediate-aged students (grades seven and eight) in the context of Ontario schools, mostly in inclusive classrooms. Case 1 (No IEPs?) provides an overview of what needs and challenges can be present in a complex, inclusive grade seven classroom, even if there are no students who have Individual Education Plans. This case includes students with a range of ongoing health-related needs, such as severe allergies, scoliosis, and cystic fibrosis, as well as a student with a temporary issue that needs environmental accommodations—a severe bone break. Case 2 (My New Best Friend Is a Service Dog) tells a story about Rochelle, a grade eight student with ASD, who gets a service dog during the school year. The service dog is intended to help with Rochelle's elopement difficulties, and will become a member of the school community—though not without a bumpy transition process around policies and procedures. Case 3 (Henrik's New Accommodations) is focused on a grade six student who is injured in a hockey game. Due to the resulting traumatic brain injury, he has seizures, chronic pain, difficulty sleeping, and trouble with verbal expressive language. This case is about not only Henrik's adjustment but also the new ways his peers learn to communicate, and the accommodations that support him. Case 4 (Peyton's Passions) tells the tale of Peyton, a grade eight student with AD/HD and a learning disability who struggles with receptive learning, and excels in kinesthetic-based learning. Her team has been attempting to support her needs with assistive technology. Peyton is highly resistant, but her teachers and parents persist with brainstorming additional methods to use technology for teaching and learning. In Case 5 (Jami and His Assistive Tech), grade eight student Jami is diagnosed with an LD and struggles in both expressive and receptive language. Jami's teacher carefully documents his needs and pursues assistive technology to help accommodate his academic work in an inclusive way.

Each case in Chapter 3 includes a range of brief response questions and in-depth response questions; resources, figures, and templates are included as needed. Integrated into each case are a range of keywords, which are defined in the margins, as well as in a glossary at the end of the book. Suggested readings, websites, articles, and multimedia are found at the end of the chapter, along with chapter references.

Case 1: No IEPs?

"Are you serious? No IEPs at all? Not one?"

"That's what I was told."

I sat back in my chair. "Well, that's kind of unusual," I said, with a slight frown. "In fact, I can hardly believe it!" Visions of effective classroom management immediately danced in my head with glee. "Usually by grade seven, we get all sorts of students with IEPs in our classrooms. At least, that is what I have experienced in the three years that I have been a substitute teacher in many, many classrooms around our board. Of course, having IEPs is not a *bad* thing—just a complicated thing!"

"I don't know what to say," responded the teacher candidate assigned to my current classroom. "But it seems to be true!"

This was my first partial day in grade seven as a long-term occasional teacher. I had received the call this morning from my now-principal, who informed me that the grade seven teacher had headed off on maternity leave—necessarily—earlier than planned, fairly unexpectedly. I had walked into the school around 3 PM, just as the final wrap-up for the day was happening. *It seems like a busy and happy school*, I had thought, as I noted the presence of teachers, administrators, and what I figured was the resource teacher, talking and laughing with students, as well as giving some pretty firm instructions on what to do next. *Definitely an organized chaos*, my thoughts had continued, *which I like*.

I had found my new classroom down at the end of an H-shaped set of corridors, in what was referred to as the "intermediate wing." I took a quick peek in the window inserted into the hall door, and saw a fairly traditional set-up of desks in rows, with a scruffy couch off to the side. *It looks like business as usual*, I considered with satisfaction, and then knocked. After I was welcomed into the grade seven class and waved a little over-heartily at my soon-to-be students by way of initial introductions, I left the substitute teacher to do her busy thing, and I spied another adult over in the corner, flipping through a binder with avid attention, making notes throughout. *Interesting*, I thought, taking a mental note. *Who is that?* Another noteworthy thing I noticed, looking around the room for the first time, while standing unobtrusively off to the side, was a row of what looked to be **profiles** of students on the wall, printed on bright orange card stock. *Another thing to ask about*, I thought. As I moved slowly through the classroom, with my eyes roving about to absorb the students and their surroundings, I tripped a little and caught myself. Looking to the side after the inevitable rise and fall of teenage giggles, I noticed a walker-type mechanism tangled with my feet. Extricating myself, I moved more carefully to the back, and arrived by the teacher's desk just when the bell rang. Immediately, any possible interest in me dissipated, and the students competed with one another to leave as quickly as possible—for the most part—excepting the student with the walker and another using crutches with an evident air cast on her foot.

After a short conversation with the substitute teacher, where I explained that I would be supporting the classroom for the remainder of the school year, and

Profiles (student)
A planning and information-gathering tool used to outline a student's strengths, needs, and the methods of assessment and instruction best suited to the student's learning-style preferences and needs.

where I was introduced to the "other adult" in the room (a teacher candidate)—the one still flipping through a binder—I asked for a summary of the classroom to help me get started on my planning. Although the substitute teacher headed out fairly quickly due to a family commitment, the teacher candidate stayed around to talk. She started off with the basics.

"We have 29 students, give or take, but since we have a fairly transient population with a good deal of poverty," she told me, "we usually end up with around 23 or 25 students every day."

That's when she told me about the IEPs, and that's when I began to get excited about the idea of a classroom that perhaps was not as complex as some of my other ones had been so far in the first few years of my career. I imagined being able to plan field trips with comfort and ease, track and field day without special activities, and classroom instruction without remembering accommodations. My imagination kind of went wild all on its own until a bump on my hand brought me back to reality. The teacher candidate had nudged her binder over to my side of the table.

"We have been working on this for you in the past few weeks. It's not quite all ready, but I think it will give you a really good overview of the class. We have information about every student, but we started with the profiles first."

"Profiles . . . ?" I asked, feeling a little out of touch. "What are profiles?"

"These are profiles!" she pointed out, and I followed her finger right to those orange papers I had noticed on the wall. We got up and walked over together to examine them in more detail.

Elizabeth-Christina was the first one, with her photo beside her name, with her birthdate, grade, teacher, and emergency contact information. Under this was a list of bullet points:

- Mild **scoliosis**
  · Needs stretching breaks
- **Allergic** to shellfish
  · Carries an **EpiPen**
  · Emergency EpiPen below

Under this was a pouch attached to the wall with what appeared to be industrial strength hook-and-loop tape, holding what I assumed to be her medical device.

My eyes moved to the left. I saw Iva, next. Iva's profile had these points:

- Mild **cystic fibrosis**
  · Medication required
  · Tires easily
  · Frequent breaks required
  · Unlimited bathroom access

"We have our own bathroom," gestured the teacher candidate to an open door on one wall of the classroom. Only half-listening, absorbed in my material, I nodded and continued reading.

Scoliosis A condition that leads to an abnormal curvature of the spine either to the left or to the right, affecting the chest and the lower back.

Allergy An immune response by the body to a substance that the body is hypersensitive to. Reaction severity can range from mild swelling or difficulty breathing to vomiting, pain, asphyxiation, and death.

EpiPen A brand of auto-injector that contains epinephrine; used as a first-line treatment for severe allergic reactions that may be life threatening.

Cystic fibrosis A multi-system disorder that produces a variety of symptoms including persistent cough with mucous, wheezing, and shortness of breath; frequent chest infections; bowel disturbances; and weight loss or failure to gain weight despite increased appetite. Occurs when a child inherits, from both parents, the gene mutation responsible for cystic fibrosis.

IVA

25 May
Contact: 703-556-1234

- (Mild) Cystic Fibrosis
- Medication required
- Tires easily
- Frequent breaks required
- Unlimited bathroom access

Figure 3.1.1 Iva's Profile
Source: Author-generated, photo used with permission of author.

Peeter, I read. I turned back to the teacher candidate. "It says here that Peeter uses a scooter?" I inquired, curiously.

"Um, yes, well, it's kind of a scooter. I am not sure how to describe it. He had a really bad complex ankle break earlier this month playing, and they said that the scooter would be a lot better for him than using crutches while he recovers, as it's going to be a while. He's actually pretty fast on it. You should see him belting around the gym! In fact, you will get to see it, pretty soon, I'd say! And, that's about it for our profiles."

Together, we returned to sit down at the table, where the teacher candidate opened the binder to the front. "We have the profiles in your binder, too, right here at the front where you can find them easily. We made profiles of all the students in the class to help you out with all of their individual strengths, needs—and any **red flags**. If you look down the side here"—the teacher candidate ran her finger along

Red flag An indication of when it may be necessary to seek advice or assistance, or to engage in intervention.

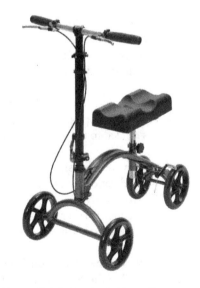

Figure 3.1.2 Peeter's Knee Scooter

the far end of the ream of paper—"you can see that we have attached little red flags for any emergency-type situations—or ones that can easily cause an emergency." She closed it up and passed it to me. "What else do you want to know?" she asked, clearly endlessly patient and enjoying her time in this classroom.

"I am not sure what else I want to know or need to know at this point," I answered, "but I am pretty sure of what I have learned. Now I know that 'No IEPs' does not mean 'no needs.' My first lesson in this classroom is already learned!"

Brief Response Questions

1. What accommodations would Peeter need in the school environment, including during gym class? Create a list of three to five possibilities.
2. What resource would you suggest is helpful for supporting students with cystic fibrosis in the school environment?
3. How do you think an item like a knee scooter could be best placed in the classroom environment to support both the student's mobility and a safe classroom space? Explain.
4. How would you accommodate stretching breaks in the classroom? Briefly explain what steps you would use.
5. How would you accommodate unlimited bathroom access in the classroom? Briefly explain what steps you would use.
6. Would you suggest the use of special jewellery to your families, such as the MedicAlert, or Allerbling?

In-Depth Response Questions

1. Do you agree that none of these students should have IEPs? Why or why not? Support your response with Ministry- or board-based legislation, policy, or processes.
2. If you developed an IEP for Iva, what would it look like? Describe any strengths/needs, accommodations, modifications, and/or alternative programs that you would use.
3. Locate a school-based policy around EpiPens, in your own board, or in an Ontario school. Summarize this policy noting one or more "Aha!" moments for you from reading this document.
4. Do you think that the use of profiles with health information posted publicly on a classroom wall could potentially violate any privacy and/or health-care legislation? Explain, with reference to related provincial or federal legislation.
5. Either (a) develop a one-page handout for parents around shellfish allergies, (b) create a detailed list of essential information it should include, or (c) find an example and analyze its elements.

Case 2: My New Best Friend Is a Service Dog

October: Grade 8

"He's really cool," said Janika, Rochelle's next-door neighbour and also her best friend at school, before she started back munching on the baby carrots in her lunch. Talking through carroty shreds, she continued. "Well, you know how Rochelle has autism and can get really freaked out and sometimes she tries to run away? The dog kind of stops dead still and Rochelle can't get away at all. Then when Rochelle calms down, she doesn't want to get away any more. She has a special kind of dog food and they have to take really good extra-special care of her—even clean her ears."

"And does she have a name?" inquired the teacher, who was sitting across from Janika for a moment while rotating through various classrooms on lunch duty. "Oh yeah, it's Rocky, because she is as heavy as a rock when she doesn't let Rochelle run off. At least that's what I heard. Also I am pretty sure she's Rochelle's new best friend. She hasn't come to the school yet, but she has been on lots of visits to the house." Janika went back to eating.

The intermediate division—located in a portable "pod" in the yard of the main school—was buzzing with discussion about Rochelle's new **service dog**. Only Janika—and of course Rochelle—had met Rocky, but she was supposed to be arriving tomorrow. The students were pretty excited about it, and even the teacher joined in with happy anticipation, but other conversations and plans around Rocky's arrival had not been so smooth.

> **Service dog**   A dog trained to do work or perform tasks for the benefit of an individual with a physical, sensory, psychiatric, or mental disability. For individuals with ASD, service dogs perform repetitive, non-verbal actions that are understood by these individuals, and also provide a sense of comfort.

Certified Service Dogs for Autism

Since 1996, National Service Dogs (NSD) has been training Labrador and Golden Retrievers to assist children and families living with autism. NSD is proud to be the first school in the world to provide this service to families with children who have autism.

Over the last 20 years, NSD has placed over 300 Certified Service Dogs across Canada and has helped various training schools around the world develop their own autism programs.

Benefits include:
- Increased Safety Levels: Children with autism have a high tendency to bolt and have no concept of danger. Our dogs are tethered to the child and trained to take commands from the parent. When the child goes to run, the dogs are given a "halt" command, anchoring the child from going any further than the tether allows.
- Improved Socialization: Having the safety and security of a Certified Service Dog allows families to get out of the house and participate in new experiences on a more regular basis. When individuals see the child with their Certified Service Dog, it sparks interest and questions that engage the child and encourages the child to talk about their dog.
- Suppressed Behavioural Outbursts: Individuals with autism have a difficult time transitioning to new environments and often experience sensory overload. Their

Certified Service Dog remains a constant in their life and allows them to focus on their dog as opposed to their environment, which often assists with suppressing behavioural issues. The dog also acts as a tactile distraction to redirect the child to a more positive behaviour.

Figure 3.2.1 Certified Service Dogs for Autism
Source: Adapted from National Service Dogs, 2012.
http://www.nsd.on.ca/programs/certified-service-dogs-for-autism/

October: Grade 7

Rochelle's school had started fundraising for service dogs a long time ago—years ago—as part of their school-wide plan to help others. They had been learning about being good citizens and helping others and had decided to donate any funds to help out with service dogs. But it was still a bit of a surprise to the principal when Rochelle's father first came to the school to talk to him about bringing a service dog into the school. "Rochelle is getting a service dog in a few months," he had told the principal. "Just in time for grade eight. One of the things that her dog will help with is with running away—what they call **elopement**. We have already had a number of lessons with the service dogs and even had a few trial runs with Rochelle. We have tried out the tether, and it's pretty amazing. We have actually been able to go on a few outings and didn't even need both parents to intervene when Rochelle was having unsafe behaviours. Plus, everyone comes up to Rochelle and talks to Rocky and then they talk to her, too, so her social and communication skills are having a workout. In any case, I brought you some information to read over, because I know

> **Elopement** A common trait of individuals with Autism Spectrum Disorders where they leave or "run away from" a safe, familiar area in order to cope with stress of external stimuli.

Service Dogs and Children with Autism Spectrum Disorders

Why is the issue important?
With the rising number of children diagnosed with ASD in the school system, there is also increasing advocacy from families, advocates and professional groups for appropriate and individualized educational programs for these students. Training service dogs to help individuals with autism is relatively new, but has been receiving growing attention over the past two decades. The service dogs are trained to respond and follow commands given by the child's caregiver (parent or legal guardian) while at home and in the community or by an educator while at school.

While there is little research on how these animals affect children with autism, families report that they have seen improvements in their children who struggle with self-stimulatory behaviors, impulsive running, anxiety and communication challenges. National Service Dogs, an organization established in 1996 in Cambridge, Ontario (the first organization in Canada to provide this service) has graduated over 170 autism service dogs across Canada. The organization claims the trained dogs increase safety levels and impede bolting when tethered to the child.

continued

In addressing a parent's request for a service dog as an accommodation for their child with ASD, schools should not only be aware of the research, but also be mindful of possible legal implications associated with such an accommodation. Although there are no reported court cases in Canada, two elementary school students with autism have recently won court orders in Illinois allowing their dogs to accompany them to school. The courts argue that a person with autism would be considered a person with a disability; and a service animal is any guide dog, signal dog or other animal individually trained to provide assistance to someone with a disability.

Parent Perspectives

Parents and proponents of service dogs for children with autism speak to many benefits but in general delineate four areas in which a service dog can assist the family and child:

- **Safety:** The service dog acts as a physical anchor for the child with autism.
- **Independence and Public Outings:** The service dog allows the child to walk more independently of the caregiver and acts as a constant companion to the child.
- **Behaviour:** Service dogs may help modify behaviour by providing a calming influence, allowing the child to cope with transitions between places, activities, and changes in routines.
- **Community and Social Benefits:** The service dogs are seen as bridging the social gap between children with autism and others by providing opportunities for communication and assisting with the integration of children with peers and the public.

Summary and Recommendations

In light of the increasing requests by parents to have service dogs accompany their children with ASD to school and the associated legal implications, the following recommendations are provided:

1. Individual jurisdictions should seek legal advice as they consider developing policy and guidelines to address this issue.
2. It is recommended provinces/districts prepare for such requests by developing or clarifying guidelines to assist in and support decision making.
3. There are a number of issues to be considered as schools develop policies and guidelines to guide their response to requests for service dogs as an accommodation for children with ASD. These include, but are not limited to, the following:
   - Health issues such as allergies of other students and school personnel
   - Training for designated handlers in the school
   - The care and welfare of the service dog while in the school setting
   - Transportation of dog and child

- The education of staff and students concerning the purpose and protocols for interaction with the service dog
- Liability in case of harm—harm to an individual by the dog or harm incurred by the dog
- Potential risks, and costs

Figure 3.2.2 Service Dogs and Children with Autism Spectrum Disorders
Source: Excerpted with slight adaptations from Atlantic Provinces Special Education Authority & Autism in Education, 2011. http://aie.apsea.ca/info-papers.html

you probably want to make some plans, and I knew that you would be especially happy given how much you have fundraised for service dogs. Like you, we have been fundraising for a long time to make this happen." Rochelle's dad handed a copy of "Service Dogs and Children with Autism Spectrum Disorders" to the principal, an article that one of the other parents on his ASD Facebook group had suggested.

Speechless so far at this rather surprising conversation, Rochelle's principal looked from the package of papers now in her hands back to Rochelle's dad. "Thanks," he said, hesitantly, wondering what can of worms he had inadvertently opened. "I definitely want to do some planning. And I am going to start with this." He gestured by nodding down at the information package. "Thanks for stopping by and for giving us lots of time to do this well."

After Rochelle's dad left the school, the principal thought, *Now what? I don't even know of another school around here that has had a service dog. This is definitely going to be an interesting journey.* He put the information package on service dogs in his to-read folio and wrote a quick email to the board to see if the special education consultant had any experience. He also chatted with the resource teacher to see if she had any experience with writing service dogs into IEPs—and she had not. *So,* thought the principal, *we are going to need a school policy, or maybe a board policy, and we are going to have to update Rochelle's IEP and her **Behaviour Support Plan** and **safety plan** at the end of the term with this information. It seems there is a lot to consider: How will Rocky get to school? Who will give the dog water? Who will deal with its poop? What if another student is scared of dogs? What if someone is allergic to dogs? Can we find any picture books about service dogs to explain Rocky to the other students? What about all of the dog hair—is that going to be a problem? What if the other students (and staff) want to pet Rocky incessantly?*

Moving ahead, many new first steps were made in preparation for Rochelle's service dog. The principal discovered that some school boards already had service dog policies well in place, and his school board, in turn, then used some of these to help develop their policies and procedures. One of these even had a sample letter home to parents.

Behaviour Support Plan A written plan that targets the underlying purpose of undesired behaviour, replaces that behaviour with something more appropriate, and reduces or eliminates the undesired behaviour.

Safety plan A crisis-response plan designating responsibilities to staff members who are trained to intervene with students experiencing crisis. It can also be a plan developed at the school level for a student who, because of their behaviour, may pose a risk to him/herself, other students, staff, or others.

[School Letterhead]

Date:

Dear Parent/Guardian:

This letter is to inform you that there will be a Certified Service Dog in our school assisting one of our students.

This Certified Service Dog is a highly trained Certified Service Dog for our student and is able to assist in many of the routine activities which may pose some challenges for this student. This child's right to have a Certified Service Dog is protected under Human Rights legislation.

There will be information sessions at the school to integrate the Certified Service Dog into our daily routines and all our students will be instructed as to the proper procedure regarding the Certified Service Dog. They will be informed that the Certified Service Dog is a working Certified Serivce Dog and not a pet while at school.

Already, the Certified Service Dog has been a benefit to the student, and we look forward to a lot of growth and learning together.

Thank you for your understanding and support.

Sincerely,

Principal

C.C. Superintendent of Learning; Special Education; OSR

Figure 3.2.3 Sample Letter to the School Community
Source: Waterloo Catholic District School Board, 2016. https://www.intranet.durham.edu.on.ca/ Applications/DDSBPPI.nsf/0/8525751600711c4f852577de006a5b45/$FILE/Appendix%20I.pdf

Antecedent strategy
Strategy used to prevent problematic behaviours by adapting the environment, informed by previous identification of antecedents that occur prior to the behaviour.

They also listed "service dog" as an environmental accommodation in Rochelle's revised IEP, and revised her safety plan around elopement to integrate help from Rocky—a great **antecedent strategy**!

ACCOMMODATIONS

(Accommodations are assumed to be the same for all subjects, unless otherwise indicated)

Instructional Accommodations	Environmental Accommodations	Assessment Accommodations
• Chunk information • Pre-teach concepts • Use visual lists for task completion • First/then • Visual schedule • Tap desk one time as a cue to regain attention	• Preferential seating near instruction • Use of labelled bins/drawers to organize materials • Designated area in classroom for quiet/relaxing time • Use of guide dog for transitions and calming	• Oral and performance assessments when possible • Allow extra time to complete tasks

Figure 3.2.4 Rochelle's List of Accommodations, Including a Service Dog
Source: Adapted from Ontario Ministry of Education, 2004. http://www.edu.gov.on.ca/eng/general/elemsec/speced/guide/resource/iepresguid.pdf, p. 53.

Safety Plan

Student: Rochelle Flora	**OEN:** 12345678PM	**d.o.b.**

Category		

Risk of injury behaviour: • Putting self in danger • Flight risk	**Specific behaviours:** • Runs out of classroom • Leaves school building • Leaves school property
Indicators of imminent risk of injury behaviour: • Rochelle will become agitated/anxious by standing up, jumping, flapping arms, screaming, rocking. • She will then head for the nearest exit, classroom door, exit door. • She will leave school property.	**Non-physical intervention methods to be used in response to indicators:** • Verbal redirection to a safe area with service dog • Call to resource teacher or principal for backup • Clearing of audience • Use of visual cues • Initiate a walk to an alternate area with service dog • Provide a sensory tool such as service dog or weighted blanket
Reassurance & follow-up support for student: • Debrief Rochelle on her actions • Review safe and unsafe behaviour with a social script	
Responsibility for Communication with administration: Classroom Teacher Communication with agencies: Resource Teacher	**Responsibility for** Communication with Parents: Classroom Teacher

continued

Board Documentation to be completed:	Board Response:
Behaviour Logs, Data Collection *Report of Accident/Injury Form (if required)*	As per school board reporting policy • *Safe Schools Incident Reporting Forms*
Debriefing & Review Procedures for Staff: *Safety plan will be reviewed by in-school team*	**Ongoing Staff Support Plan:** • *Monitored by in-school team*

Development of the Safety Plan	
Participant	**Name(s)**
Family: *Parents*	*Mr and Ms Flora*
School Staff: *School Administrator* *Education Resource Teacher*	*Mr Bob Somba (Principal)* *Ms Nancy Ling*
Board Services: *Co-ordinator Special Education* *Autism Spectrum Disorder Consultant* *Behaviour Resource Teacher*	*Mrs Stella Bean* *Ms Lily Nay* *Mr Jay Randen*

Principal's Signature & Date	Parent's or Parents' Signature(s) & Date

Figure 3.2.5 Rochelle's Revised Safety Plan
Source: Adapted from http://www.edu.gov.on.ca/eng/general/elemsec/speced/Caring_Safe_School.pdf, p. 39, and from Niagara Catholic District School Board.

Some months of planning followed before everything was in place and everyone was just waiting to meet Rocky.

Brief Response Questions

1. Have you ever encountered an IEP that included information about a service dog? If no, why do you think not? If yes, describe it.
2. Access the National Service Dogs (Ontario) website and describe the training that service dogs receive.

3. Would you consider fundraising and/or donating funds to support the adoption of a service dog for a child with ASD? Why or why not?
4. Why do you think Rochelle's father used a resource (information paper) from a jurisdiction other than Ontario?
5. Provide one or two examples of what you think any roles and responsibilities of school-based personnel would be with a service dog on-site during the school day.

In-Depth Response Questions

1. How is a service dog for students with ASD different from or the same as a service dog for students who are blind or low vision? Briefly explain or use a Venn diagram to show similarities/differences.
2. Do you think that the use of service dogs for students with ASD in schools is supported by any disability and/or human rights legislation? Explain, with reference to related provincial or federal legislation and/or policies.
3. Read and/or watch and react to a CTV news article entitled "Local MPP Introduces Private Member's Bill for Service Dogs in Public Places" (6 June 2016) found online at http://kitchener.ctvnews.ca/local-mpp-introduces-private-member-s-bill-for -service-dogs-in-public-places-1.2933675
   How might the process and/or attitudes at Rochelle's school have been different had Rochelle's principal read this news item during his planning process?
4. The "Letter to the School Community" does not include any invitation or consultation to talk about issues like severe dog allergies in other children. Develop a revised letter, including any essential issues that you think should be included (e.g., allergies, fear, feeding, petting, etc.).

Case 3: Henrik's New Accommodations

Guest contributors: Sheri Mallabar & Megan Henning
(MEd Candidates, Brock University, St Catharines, ON)

Chronic pain Any pain lasting more than 12 weeks. It may start from an initial injury, or there may be an ongoing cause, such as an illness. Fatigue, decreased appetite, mood changes, and other health problems including those related to limited movements (such as reduced flexibility, strength, and stamina) often accompany chronic pain.

Sleep disorder Difficulty initiating or maintaining sleep, or consistent disturbances in sleep patterns, or excessive feelings of sleepiness.

Seizures A short disruption, lasting from several seconds to over five minutes, in brain activity that interferes with its function, impacting behaviour and/or sensory function, such as movement, posture, memory, consciousness, vision, or hearing.

Traumatic brain injury Caused by an object or force violently impacting the head, or piercing through the skull and damaging brain tissue, often as a result of an accident or assault. A wide variety of short- and long-term symptoms include pain, memory impairment, sleep disruption, confusion, fatigue, nausea, mood swings, sensory impairments, and disorientation.

As I enter the classroom and look around at my peers, I notice everyone is happy—hugging, laughing, and sharing stories of their summer adventures. I see that Sheena's hair is different. It is longer now. It hangs below her shoulders. I scan the classroom looking for other familiar faces. I think I see Pierre, who appears to be towering over the group. When did Remi's braces come off? *Everyone seems thrilled to be starting grade eight, and I just feel surrounded by a room full of strangers.*

I shouldn't feel that way, though. After all, I've known everyone here since kindergarten. Mylika actually lived next door for almost five years! But I guess a lot can change when you miss a year of school. It seems like nothing has been quite the same since that October hockey tournament during grade six.

My mom was always concerned about me playing with the Ravens, a Junior B hockey team, whose players were all at least two years older than me. But moms are always worried and not many grade six students get the opportunity to play that level of hockey. I'm pretty sure my dad finally convinced her, actually. I loved the feeling that I got as I swerved between players twice my size. I couldn't control my smile as I racked up points and eventually became the second-leading scorer on my team.

During one particular tournament against a team from Vancouver, the competitive nature of both teams was super high. They were looking to move onto the finals as they usually do, and we were in overtime looking for one goal. My team hadn't competed in finals in over three years and my teammates were just as anxious for a chance at winning—anything. I sped up to receive the breakaway pass from our left wing and was rushing down the right side . . . and that's when it happened. I felt the hit from behind first, then my neck rolled backwards only to be jolted forward until my head met the glass. I remember my mother crying about the lack of rules regarding hits at this age; however, even in my state, I knew it was an unintentional accident. I don't blame anyone for what had happened that day, even though I know this is why everything changed.

Returning to school wasn't possible at first, between the **chronic pain**, **sleep disorder**, and **seizures**; I wasn't able to leave home for a long time. While I wasn't able to attend school my parents wanted to be sure I did not fall behind. With the help of private educators, special education tutors, and teachers from the school, I was able to complete my required coursework for grade seven.

When I started to feel better, my doctors determined I could return to school after the summer for grade eight. My mother was nervous about my speech, my hearing ability, and what all the doctors referred to as my processing ability; these were all things that resulted from the **traumatic brain injury** and would not disappear like the other short-term effects. However, after a lot of convincing, my mother agreed that it would be best for me.

My parents met with the principal, learning resource teacher, classroom teacher, and counsellor before school started, to discuss the kind of help I would need (like brain breaks, extended deadlines, adapted assignments, and stuff like that), all things designed to keep my stress levels down. One of the things we have been practising is using sign language (ASL). I was nervous about using ASL with my peers; however, I knew that it would be more effective than trying to have them decipher the slurred words coming out of my mouth. I had always thought that ASL was only used by people who couldn't hear; however, one of my therapists explained that it might also be helpful in my situation even though I still have hearing abilities. She said that since I had been having trouble communicating through speech, I might find myself able to communicate more fluently through sign. I later learned that I was actually rather fortunate to have damaged my left hemisphere, as it is the right hemisphere that is responsible for most social communication. They even suggested that we could implement a plan for me to teach my peers some ASL so that I wouldn't struggle making out their speech with my decreased hearing abilities.

As I look back to the group where Pierre is clearly making a joke that everyone is laughing at, I try to decide how to approach my friends that I haven't seen in so long. The morning bell saves me from having to make that decision. Everyone heads towards the neat rows of desks. I quietly move to the front, where my homeroom teacher had asked me to sit on one of my many school visits this summer. He wanted to ensure I didn't have any difficulty hearing him during class lessons.

The morning announcements must be on because it's 9 AM. Among classroom chatter, fellow students start cheering at something they heard, but I'm not sure what it is. I look over to Pierre who mouths, "I'll tell you after." It turns out this wasn't the only problem I would have during my first week back. I started to question whether it was a good idea to return to school after I had to remind Mr Oakshire to turn the closed captioning on during a science video. It's not like he isn't accommodating though; he does his best to face me when speaking, to provide visual copies of instructions, and to find programs to share the announcements on visually. I guess I just thought after months of planning my return, it would be a little easier.

I began sharing keywords and phrases with the class using ASL but quickly noticed that they never talked about their weekend, or games they like, or movies they saw because they were only remembering basic signs like "Hi!" "How are you?" "Lunch time." *I can't really blame them; it took me over a year to learn all of the signs I use.* Mr Oakshire must have noticed my frustration with the lack of communication between myself and my peers and approached me with some suggestions as to what we could try next. He said that during his meeting with the resource teacher, the idea of an iPad communication app came up. Apparently this would help me to communicate more complex ideas through typing and saved messages. It would even allow my peers to type into the app to share ideas or conversation. *I was willing to try anything at this point; I just wanted to be able to talk to my friends like before.*

American Sign Language (ASL)
The primary visually perceived language in North America, it uses hand gestures, their placement relative to the body, as well as facial expressions and other body movements to communicate meaning.

ACCOMMODATIONS
(Accommodations are assumed to be the same for all subjects, unless otherwise indicated)

Instructional Accommodations	Environmental Accommodations	Assessment Accommodations
	• *Preferential seating (near window to allow for natural light), near instruction* • *Non-fluorescent lighting at least 50% of the day* • *Visual schedule posted in classroom* • **FM system** • *Study carrel* • *Use of labelled bins/drawers to organize materials* • *Designated area in classroom for quiet/relaxing time*	

Figure 3.3.1 List of Environmental Accommodations

Source: Adapted from Ontario Ministry of Education, 2004. http://www.edu.gov.on.ca/eng/general/elemsec/speced/guide/resource/iepresguid.pdf, p. 53. © Queen's Printer for Ontario. Reproduced with permission.

Frequency Modulation (FM) system A method of transmitting sound from a transmitter (worn by the speaker or teacher) to the listener's (or student's) hearing aid or other receiver in order to amplify a particular sound for the listener.

Weeks later, I began communicating with my friends. We were able to talk about the game that we watched on TV the night before. My friends started telling me about what they did on the weekends. I was happy there for a while. Then one day, Erika, who I had been talking to quite regularly (I guess I had developed a little crush on her), typed the question I had been afraid someone would ask. As I looked down at the iPad, I read, "Henrik, how is your head injury different from a concussion?" *I kind of figured she might ask this; I knew she had had a concussion from soccer last year.* I thought for a minute about how to best answer her question. I then began to type everything I had learned since my accident. I explained how concussions generally have short-term effects, how my brain injury has permanently altered my speech, and how I was unconscious for over an hour, whereas most people who have concussions may have been unconscious for less than thirty minutes or not at all. Erika smiled and thanked me for answering her question. We've become good friends since then. I think my explanation helped my friends understand that I was still the same person as before; I just had to communicate and do some things differently than I had before.

I decided that Mr Oakshire's idea for the communication app on the iPad turned out to work pretty well. He even found a program that allowed everyone to type and brainstorm with rapid-fire responses showing on the Smart Board screen. I was able to see what my friends were saying. Mr Oakshire also rearranged our classroom so that all of the students faced each other instead of rows facing the front. This meant that during verbal discussions, I could see each of them and really focus on what my peers were saying.

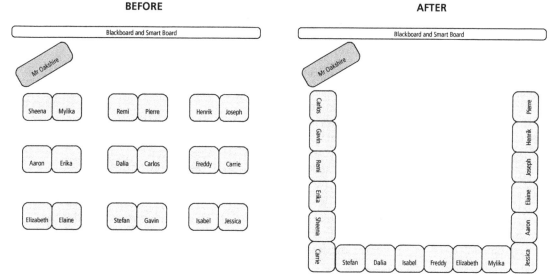

Figure 3.3.2 Mr Oakshire's Classroom: Before and After
Source: Created by guest contributors Mallabar & Henning.

My mom was really concerned that the academic aspect of school would be a struggle for me. She talked about how I would need an IEP and other stuff. It was difficult for me to tell my mom that I was more worried about reconnecting with my friends than I was about homework. As it turns out, Mr Oakshire's strategies had positive impacts for both my mom and myself. And I had my friends back. *Everything else is just icing.*

Brief Response Questions

1. Review the list of symptoms provided in "Acquired Brain Injury in the Classroom: Promoting Awareness" (Bennett, Good, & Zinga, 2000), found at http://professionallyspeaking.oct.ca/june_2000/acquired.htm
   Is Henrik exhibiting any of the symptoms? If so, which ones?
2. Find and share another Ontario or Canadian site for teaching and learning about acquired brain injury—from the field of education, health, government, and/or advocacy group(s).
3. What do you think of the way Mr Oakshire rearranged the classroom environment? Would you make other changes? Why or why not?
4. Find and share a professional development activity around acquired brain injury that you might like to attend.
5. Research and share information about an iPad app specific to communication that could help a student like Henrik.

continued

In-Depth Response Questions

1. Henrik was asked about how a traumatic brain injury is different from a concussion. Apart from what Henrik explained, research at least three other ways that they differ and explain these three (or more) differences in detail.
2. Clearly, Henrik is highly invested in ensuring that his friendships are intact. Do you agree with this emphasis—or do you feel his academic needs are more important? Discuss.
3. Download the *Ontario Brain Injury Association's Impact Report* (2012) (http://obia.ca/wp-content/uploads/2013/01/ImpactReportOnline-Dec2012.pdf) and read the section related to caregivers (pp. 118–28). Do you think that any of this relates to Henrik's parents? Write a summary about caregivers and acquired brain injury, and apply it to Henrik's parents.
4. Develop a transition plan for Henrik, using the following template. Be sure to include at least five goal areas. Think about including goals that relate to the physical domain of development, considering Henrik's love for physical, team, and sports activities.

Transition Plan

Student's name _____ OEN/MIN _____

Specific Goal(s) for Transition to _____

_____

_____

_____

_____

Action to be taken:	Responsibility of:	To be completed by:

Figure 3.3.3 Transition Plan

Source: Adapted from Ontario Ministry of Education, 2004. http://www.edu.gov.on.ca/eng/general/elemsec/speced/guide/resource/iepresguid.pdf, p. 57.

5. Choose a course typical for Henrik's grade. Would you consider modifying this course? Why or why not? Who should be involved in this decision? Discuss both the short- and long-term outcomes of each possible choice in detail.

Case 4: Peyton's Passions

Peyton's uncle nicknamed her "the bouncer" when she was four years old, and it was a nickname that stuck, continuing to fit Peyton even as she grew into adolescence. As a 13-year-old teenager entering the second month of grade eight, Peyton still loves to bounce, though the bouncing had changed from a more physical spinning around her homemade backyard gymnastic bar and cartwheeling down the street to chat with neighbours and playmates to a more cognitive bouncing from activity to activity.

From Peyton's teachers' point of view, she appears quite incapable of paying attention to anything that doesn't interest her to an almost-obsessive level. Like her earlier childhood experiences, this can be anything involving gymnastics—or dance. She still takes lessons in both and is on any related school teams that she can find. But new in the last few years, she is also extremely involved in a social life that revolves around gaming and digital devices.

With two parents in a high-paying medical field and Peyton as an only child, it hasn't been difficult for Peyton's needs and wants to be accommodated with the latest video game systems, tablet technology, and, of course, the ubiquitous cell phone: every teenager's number-one necessity. This seems to work fine at home most of the time—except when it's time for homework to be done—but is causing an increasing number of problems at school. Peyton is "that student" who was caught so many times with her cell phone propped between her body and her desk, typing rapidly with both thumbs, that she now has to turn in her cell phone when she gets to school in the morning and pick it back up when school is dismissed. Even though Peyton is almost ready for high school, her parents remain highly involved in her life at school, continually collaborating and co-operating with the school staff in trying to work out what they call Peyton's "little foibles."

"We think she is going to end up doing a kinesiology degree before medical school," one of her parents had said at the last school meeting to try to sort out Peyton's attention issues in the school environment and to revise her IEP. "She is clearly skilled at using her body, and really seems to have an intuitive grasp of how muscles work together in herself and others. She actually started volunteering as a Kindergym coach on Saturday mornings, and you should see how far she takes the little ones in what they can do on the beam and in floor exercise. Not to mention the trampoline! It's so good to see her in her element. She has such a sharp focus when she is at the dance or gymnastics studio, with such a fine-tuned understanding of how to manipulate actions and reactions into what works. There hasn't been one injury—even a minor one—in the Kindergym classes so far. She might not listen to instructions herself, but the kids sure listen to her giving them!"

Peyton's grade seven homeroom teacher, who was listening in an enthralled way to the passionate description of a Peyton that she has never seen in her own classroom, thought, *What?* Then she responded, "What you are describing fits in really well with what we believe here at the school: we believe in a **strengths-based approach**. Obviously, we are only getting to know Peyton, but we have seen what is on her IEP, and we have watched her in class, and the lists of her strengths and needs that came from her last IPRC meeting still seem to fit. It looks like it has been updated regularly and carefully since grade four. So what do you think?" Peyton's teachers and parents reviewed them together.

STUDENT'S STRENGTHS AND NEEDS

Areas of Strength	Areas of Need
Social skills	Organization
Physical education	Planning
Energy	Task completion
Enthusiasm	Assistive technology skills
*enjoys gaming, gymnastics, dance, track and field	

Figure 3.4.1 Peyton's Strengths & Needs
Source: Adapted from Ontario Ministry of Education, 2004. http://www.edu.gov.on.ca/eng/general/elemsec/speced/guide/resource/iepresguid.pdf, p. 52.

"I noticed that the last time she had a formal assessment, the results showed that she is very bright and obviously capable of understanding academics, but that she was also diagnosed with an LD and AD/HD, and identified as 'Communication: Learning Disability' soon afterward. All her screening and her medical appointments are up to date. It says here that her biggest barrier is with getting information *in*. It seems that once Peyton 'gets' something—a gymnastics move, a math problem, or a ballet pose—she really gets it. But she has to see it—a lot—or actually do it. Or both. I see that Peyton's pediatrician recommended medication but you made a family decision to decline it, and that he is also concerned about depression and/or anxiety. It looks like you considered the option of Peyton attending a **provincial school** last year, and also considered **home-schooling**, but didn't move forward with these options."

"That sounds right," said Peyton's mother, making eye contact with Peyton's father. "When she was younger and before she was diagnosed, I used to have to show her an almost full-on dramatic play to get school concepts to sink in at home. I made her playroom doors into a huge chalkboard, and I put up a felt board on another wall to help her use her **kinesthetic** skills to learn new concepts. That has all kind of fallen by the wayside, now, as she has moved on to her video games and

Strengths-based approach Emphasizes one's abilities as opposed to any difficulties or deficits. This approach is grounded in the belief that all individuals have unique potential, and that their personal realities must be understood in order to be successfully inclusive.

Provincial school School that provides province-wide programs and services for students who are deaf, are hard of hearing, are blind, have low vision, are deaf-blind, and/or have learning disabilities.

Home-schooling A system in which students do not attend formal publicly funded education; rather, they learn curriculum-based information at home from someone who may or may not be an Ontario Certified Teacher.

Kinesthetic learning Learning through movement and position of, and sensory input from, the body. Use of physical involvement and movement as part of the learning environment can engage those with a kinesthetic learning style.

WordQ Word-prediction software that supports literacy and writing through a variety of features. Word lists, text-to-speech, language dictionaries, thesaurus, and suggestions based on similar spelling and sounds allow the software to be adapted to suit individual needs.

ASSESSMENT DATA

List relevant educational, medical/health (hearing, vision, physical, neurological), psychological, speech/language, occupational, physiotherapy, and behavioural assessments.

Information Source	Date	Summary of Results
Psychoeducational Assessment	4 November	Full psychoeducational assessment complete. Summary report said "Peyton's results are characteristic of a learning disability."
Speech/Language Assessment	19 October	All results now in the average range. Suggested an updated visit to the audiologist.
Medical Report	27 July	Diagnosed with AD/HD by the family doctor.

Figure 3.4.2 Peyton's Assessment Summary

Source: Adapted from Ontario Ministry of Education, 2004. http://www.edu.gov.on.ca/eng/general/elemsec/speced/guide/resource/iepresguid.pdf, p. 52.

LOG OF PARENT/STUDENT CONSULTATION AND STAFF REVIEW/UPDATING

Date	Activity (Indicate parent/student consultation or staff review)	Outcome
April	Met with parents to discuss year so far and make suggestions for goals, referrals, and interventions for next year (e.g., mental health referral).	Excellent meeting. Decided on video modelling and focusing on keyboarding skills.
March	Discussed potential options for placement next year prior to yearly IPRC meeting.	No change to placement desired by family.
October	Discussed trialing assistive tech software with student and family.	Tried for two weeks but student did not like these options.

Figure 3.4.3 Peyton's Parent Log

Source: Adapted from Ontario Ministry of Education, 2004. http://www.edu.gov.on.ca/eng/general/elemsec/speced/guide/resource/iepresguid.pdf, p. 56.

electronics. And you know what it's like. Whenever we try and nudge her a different way, she says that she hates her life, and asks us why she was born. That kind of teenage melodrama."

"Yes," responded the teacher, with a wry smile. "We know. We get a similar reaction if we ask her to do anything different from what she thinks the rest of the class is doing—even though we have students with all sorts of various strengths and needs doing all types of differing tasks. When we trialed her with a laptop and some assistive technology programs like **WordQ**, we were told that we must hate her and asked why we were picking on her. I am sure you understand that none of that is actually happening. But, of course, we have referred her to our mental health supports, as well, as we want to make sure we take everything seriously and get Peyton any supports that are available for her."

Video modelling
Recordings or animations of individuals performing a desired skill, including clear step-by-step instruction and cues. Often used to teach individuals with disabilities a variety of social, academic, or functional skills.

Flipped classroom
Teachers create instructive videos and interactive lessons for at-home learning and review. Students watch and complete the material at home, and then do activities, homework-style problems, or collaborative learning on the studied concept while in the classroom—"flipping" the common instructional approach.

Function (of behaviour) The reasons(s) why a student engages in a particular behaviour. The accepted functions of behaviour are attention, escape, tangible, and sensory—or a complex combination of these.

"So we have been talking together as an in-school team, and we think that Peyton is at an important juncture where she needs to start figuring out where she wants to go in high school—and beyond high school—and to really start to self-advocate for her needs, rather than try to avoid and escape from any demands or supports that are provided. But we also think it's really important to get buy-in from Peyton by figuring out how to work with her strengths, and what she enjoys."

"I don't think anyone could argue with any of that," Peyton's dad jumped in. "In fact, if you have any hints for us, I'd love to hear them!"

"Well, in fact, we do have a few ideas that might help. First, we were thinking that we need to start encouraging and teaching Peyton to use computer technology as a teaching and learning tool, rather than simply for leisure and entertainment. Then, we were thinking that maybe we could get Peyton involved in using **video modelling**—with new concepts and skills we need her to learn, but also using this technique for her own coaching and skill-building in the studio. As well, a few of our intermediate teachers are thinking about trialing the **flipped classroom** approach for one of the social studies classes. And, last, we all think that Peyton needs to learn to keyboard efficiently and effectively with all 10 fingers so she can get things *before* she gets frustrated. What do you think? And, more importantly, what would Peyton think?"

Brief Response Questions

1. What other school-based support services might be helpful for Peyton?
2. List two or three examples of other ways that kinesthetic learners like Peyton could be supported in the school, home, and/or community.
3. What do you think is the **function** of Peyton's problem behaviour (i.e., task refusal)? Why?
4. Define self-advocacy in your own words, using an academic, professional, and/or governmental source as your foundation (and include that source).
5. Peyton's team appears to focus on a strengths-based approach. How might such an approach help Peyton—or other students?

In-Depth Response Questions

1. List and discuss at least one way which assistive technology software could be used in an inclusive manner in the school and/or classroom.

2. Either share an anecdote of how you have experienced a flipped classroom approach, or do some research and develop an explanation of how the approach might work in one of your previously taught lessons or in an upcoming lesson plan.
3. Find a research paper showing positive outcomes of video modelling, and write your own one-page summary of this research project and its results.
4. How do you predict that Peyton will react to these "ideas that might help"? Provide a rationale.
5. Each Ontario IEP has a section for logging parent/student consultation. Develop five entries that might exist in Peyton's IEP, and write a paragraph to explain why you chose these as possible examples.

LOG OF PARENT/STUDENT CONSULTATION AND STAFF REVIEW/UPDATING

Date	Activity (Indicate parent/student consultation or staff review)	Outcome

Figure 3.4.4 Parent/Student Consultation
Source: Adapted from Ontario Ministry of Education, 2004. http://www.edu.gov.on.ca/eng/general/elemsec/speced/guide/resource/iepresguid.pdf, p. 56.

6. Complete a full IEP for Peyton, using the below template. Keep in mind that if you add any modified or alternative courses to any IEP, those program pages must also be added and completed.

continued

Individual Education Plan

REASON FOR DEVELOPING THE IEP

☐ Student identified as exceptional by IPRC

☐ Student not formally identified but requires special education program/services, including modified/alternative learning expectations and/or accommodations

STUDENT PROFILE

Name: _____ Gender: _____ Date of Birth: _____

School: _____

Student OEN/MIN: _____ Principal: _____

Current Grade/Special Class: _____ School Year: _____

Most Recent IPRC Date: _____ Date Annual Review Waived by Parent/Guardian: _____

Exceptionality: _____

IPRC Placement Decision (check one)

☐ Regular class with indirect support

☐ Regular class with resource assistance

☐ Regular class with withdrawal assistance

☐ Special education class with partial integration

☐ Special education class full-time

ASSESSMENT DATA

List relevant educational, medical/health (hearing, vision, physical, neurological), psychological, speech/language, occupational, physiotherapy, and behavioural assessments.

Information Source	Date	Summary of Results

STUDENT'S STRENGTHS AND NEEDS

Areas of Strength	Areas of Need

SUBJECTS, COURSES, OR ALTERNATIVE PROGRAMS TO WHICH THE IEP APPLIES

Identify each as Modified (MOD), Accommodated only (AC), or Alternative (ALT)

1. _____ ☐ MOD ☐ AC ☐ ALT 5. _____ ☐ MOD ☐ AC ☐ ALT
2. _____ ☐ MOD ☐ AC ☐ ALT 6. _____ ☐ MOD ☐ AC ☐ ALT
3. _____ ☐ MOD ☐ AC ☐ ALT 7. _____ ☐ MOD ☐ AC ☐ ALT
4. _____ ☐ MOD ☐ AC ☐ ALT 8. _____ ☐ MOD ☐ AC ☐ ALT

Elementary Program Exemptions or Secondary School Compulsory Course Substitutions

☐ Yes (provide educational rationale)   ☐ No

_____
_____

Complete for secondary students only:

Student is currently working towards attainment of the:

☐ Ontario Secondary School Diploma   ☐ Ontario Secondary School Certificate   ☐ Certificate of Accomplishment

ACCOMMODATIONS
(Accommodations are assumed to be the same for all subjects, unless otherwise indicated)

Instructional Accommodations	Environmental Accommodations	Assessment Accommodations

Individualized Equipment   ☐ Yes (list below)   ☐ No

_____   _____
_____   _____
_____   _____

continued

LOG OF PARENT/STUDENT CONSULTATION AND STAFF REVIEW/UPDATING

Date	Activity (Indicate parent/student consultation or staff review)	Outcome

The principal is legally required to ensure that the IEP is properly implemented and monitored.

This IEP has been developed according to the ministry's standards and appropriately addresses the student's strengths and needs. The learning expectations will be reviewed and the student's achievement evaluated at least once every reporting period.

_____   _____
Principal's Signature   Date

Involvement of Parent/Guardian and Student (if student is 16 or older)

I was consulted in the development of this IEP	☐ Parent/Guardian ☐ Student
I declined the opportunity to be consulted in the development of this IEP	☐ Parent/Guardian ☐ Student
I have received a copy of this IEP	☐ Parent/Guardian ☐ Student

Parent/Guardian and Student Comments:

_____
_____
_____
_____
_____

_____   _____
Parent/Guardian Signature   Date

_____   _____
Student Signature (if 16 or older)   Date

Transition Plan

Student's name _____ OEN/MIN ___*89674523*_____

Specific Goal(s) for Transition to Post-secondary Activities _____

_____

_____

_____

_____

_____

_____

Actions Required	Person Responsible for Actions	Timelines

Figure 3.4.5 Peyton's IEP

Case 5: Jami and His Assistive Tech

Jami read his invitation quickly and stuffed it into the bottom of his backpack, mingling it with other unwanted items like bits of old lunches in plastic baggies, broken glass from his "good effort" award at the last school-wide assembly, and his

You are invited to attend:

_____

#LDSBTechweek

_____

It's your chance to learn, design, and create!

Join students Grades 7–10 from across the board.

_____

Three full days of technology-based seminars and hands-on activities

Lancaster District School Board
5515 Marlin Road
Lancaster Hills, Ontario
www.landsb.net
For more info contact:
maceyred@landsb.net

MAY 4–6
LDSB TECH WEEK

Lancaster District School Board Tech Week

Join technology teachers and board staff, guest speakers from local companies, and students from all over Lancaster District for three full days of workshops and hands-on learning in many areas including gaming, robotics, social media, software and hardware applications, and learning tools.

Figure 3.5.1 Jami's Invitation to Tech Week
Source: Monique Somma (used with permission). Word art generated using http://www.wordle.net/

battered agenda, which he tried hard to never write in, just in case his mom might see that he had homework.

Whatever, he thought to himself, being sure to cram it in deeply. *This is just another way to try to make me look different. And I am not. I'm just like everyone else. Obviously.*

But Jami's grade eight teacher saw things a little differently. Just before September began, she had read his OSR, the psychoeducational report in it, his IEP, and all of the behavioural reports she also found, turning them slowly, page by page. On his IEP, she noticed (in particular) his fairly lengthy list of assessments.

Child Disability Tax Credit   A tax-free benefit of up to $2,730 per year ($227.50 per month), as of 2017, for families who care for a child under age 18 with a medically certified physical or mental disability that has lasted, or is expected to last, for a continuous period of at least 12 months.

ASSESSMENT DATA

List relevant educational, medical/health (hearing, vision, physical, neurological), psychological, speech/language, occupational, physiotherapy, and behavioural assessments..

Information Source	Date	Summary of Results
Speech/Language Assessment	Grade 8	Delays in expressive and receptive language; reading at a grade seven level for both word knowledge and comprehension; some recent gains in reading interest; phonological awareness increasing with regular resource assistance
Psychoeducational Assessment	Grade 5	Diagnosed as Learning Disabled
Occupational Therapy Report	Grade 5	Moderate difficulties in visual motor accuracy skills; mild delays in fine motor manual dexterity skills
Audiological Report	Grade 3	Mild conductive hearing loss in both ears
Pediatric Assessment	Grade 3	Conners' Rating Scale showed high impulsivity, distractibility, and poor social skills particularly with peers

Figure 3.5.2 Previous Assessments on Jami's IEP

Source: Adapted from Individual Education Plan, 2004. http://www.edu.gov.on.ca/eng/general/elemsec/speced/guide/resource/iepresguid.pdf, p. 52.

She was a little daunted by the fact that this identified student was only one of many in her group who needed similar supports, but also daunted by the in-school team recommendations that seemed to have been developed just before school ended last year—and now were in her lap, so to speak. *Hopefully all these referrals went through before the school year ended*, she thought. She then reviewed this list, too, and made some careful notes in her moleskin notebook that contained everything about her school and classroom—so far—for the coming year, one in a long line of yearly notebooks she relished as an organization system. She noted that Jami was from a single-parent family; that he lived with his mother, older sister, and his young niece; and that they were supported primarily by Ontario Works, though Jami's mother had applied for the **Child Disability Tax Credit**.

Regular classroom   Conventional classroom that all students not assigned to an alternative classroom or school attend, averaging 20–30 students with a variety of abilities and learning needs in each, and organized by grade.

School-Based Team Meeting	Date	Student/Grade
☐ Initial ☑ Follow-up	June	Jami/Grade 7

Recommendations:	Responsibility of:
1. Consult with Board Hearing Resource Teacher for review on FM system or a sound device	Resource Teacher
2. Assistive technology: WordQ and Kurzweil?	Resource Teacher
3. IEP to be updated (accommodations/modifications in oral, reading, and written language—one grade level below; ongoing resource assistance within a **regular classroom**)	Classroom Teacher
4. Meet with mother to discuss community leisure involvement	Resource Teacher and Classroom Teacher
5. Ongoing OT support to classroom teacher	Occupational Therapist

Figure 3.5.3 In-School Team Recommendations (June)
Source: Author-generated.

Sound field device
A tool that uses speakers placed throughout the classroom to project a designated speaker's voice, useful for individuals with hearing loss, learning disabilities, attentional difficulties, or developmental delays.

She made herself a similar list in her flowing script, headed it "Jami—September," and underlined it twice.

Jami—September

- *Check with School Board Hearing Resource Teacher about an FM system or maybe a **sound field device** (Jami might not like an individual system—most grade eights don't like being centred out).*

- *Check to see if we still have **Kurzweil** on our classroom computers from last year, and check to see if WordQ is still covered by the **Ontario Software Acquisition Program Advisory Committee (OSAPAC).***

- *Plan IEP meeting with the resource teacher and Jami's mother (check for accommodations related to oral and written language and assistive technology; make sure he is on the list for help from resource).*

- *Call Jami's mother to see if he is signed up for anything (Sports? Clubs? Other activities?).*

- *Email the OT to make sure she will be back visiting our classroom this year (and check that Jami is on her list, too).*

Kurzweil An educational program or application for computer or tablet that provides text-to-speech, audio notetaking, highlighting, and multi-language capabilities for students.

Ontario Software Acquisition Program Advisory Committee (OSAPAC) The provincial body that develops, licenses, and promotes digital resources for education.

Figure 3.5.4 To-Do List
Source: Author-generated.

After making these notes, she stood up, stretched, and wandered next door to the already active staffroom, letting her mind sift through planning for the busy year in her large urban school, imagining what it would be like when the 700+ students hit the hallways. On the bulletin board where professional development events, health and safety notices, and other opportunities were regularly posted, she noticed a new list of **Response to Intervention** initiatives—a model that her school started trying out last year—and, among these, some intensive instruction opportunities for assistive technology. Thinking of Jami, she took a photo with her phone's camera to save for later—just in case.

And now, with the blink of an eye, the calendar had already switched over to October. Jami was struggling mightily in most tasks with a reading or writing component—his teacher could tell this even by the look on his face and the slope of his shoulders when he was completing individual work at his desk. She had set up WordQ and Kurzweil on the two computers to the side of the class—underneath a long bank of windows—had arranged for Jami to work with the resource teacher on learning to use these programs, and had introduced them to the whole class. While a number of Jami's classmates used Kurzweil because they simply preferred to listen to their class novel instead of "just" reading it (getting that **bi-modal** input), Jami himself had been pretty resistant to using the complex software. And, as his academic difficulties increased, his problem behaviours increased, too. *It's looking like his new identification might be "Multiple" if we can't get things to calm down,* she predicted, with frustration. But, later that day, when she was catching up with emails from the board, parents, the resource teacher, and her principal, she clicked on one entitled "Don't Forget—Assistive Tech Intensive." *Right!* she recalled, and found the photo she had taken before school started. *This training would definitely be just right for Jami!* She printed off a copy for Jami to take home to consider.

That evening, Jami's mom found the invitation in his backpack. Given the seeming lack of communication from the school, she had been taking unobtrusive looks into his backpack every once in a while, and today her technique paid off. She called him over from playing on the floor with his sister's baby, waving the invitation in the air. "Why don't you go to this? It looks great! You can learn all of that computer stuff you love in just a week, and you can take a friend with you! I am definitely signing the permission form this time." Before Jami could respond, she smoothed it out, signed it, and tucked it inside his agenda. "There. And I am going to call your teacher and make sure you go, so don't try to get out of it." Jami rolled his eyes skyward and went back to playing with his niece. He figured there was no point in trying to explain to his non-tech-savvy mom that this was definitely NOT the "cool" kind of technology that he actually WANTED to learn.

On the dot of 9 AM the next day, Jami—who had "given in"—meandered over to his teacher's in-box for forms, notes, and other important pieces of communication, and flicked in his permission form, with more than a touch of derision. *Great. Now I have to pick someone to take with me.* His eyes roamed around the classroom, and he saw Rajeet. *He's the one who uses those programs all the time, "just for fun," he says. He is kind of quiet, but smart and nice. Maybe he would go. Or maybe he wouldn't.* His eyes met his teacher's eyes, but he looked away quickly. *This really sucks,* he thought, and, head down, ambled slowly back to his desk and slumped over, his chin resting heavily on his crossed arms.

Response to Intervention (RTI)
A tiered educational approach designed to provide assessment and instruction to students. At tier one, the curriculum informs assessment and instruction. If difficulties are noted, at tier two, an educator provides differentiated instruction or an intervention. If difficulties persist, at tier three, additional resources are sought to support the student's learning with more intensive, individualized interventions.

Bi-modal Two modes of instruction or learning. For example, both lectures and a mentorship program on the same topic.

Full-time special education classroom
A separate, self-contained classroom for children with physical, academic, cognitive, or social–emotional difficulties that cannot be accommodated in a regular classroom. These classrooms are legally restricted in size by Regulation 298, section 31 of the Education Act in Ontario.

Social justice Equal distribution of wealth, opportunities, and privileges within a society, including participation in the construction of reality as well as living conditions and material forms of measurement.

Brief Response Questions

1. What do you think of the term "regular" classroom? Is there a better term to use for the most common type of placement for all students, including students who are identified with exceptionalities?
2. Since Jami has a diagnosis of a learning disability, what identification will the IPRC likely have given to him?
3. Briefly explain one or two of the main differences between a diagnosis and an identification, using an example of Jami or a fictional/non-identifiable student.
4. Why might Jami's identification change to "Multiple"? Explain.
5. Do you think that the fact that Jami doesn't want to attend this training will impact the outcomes of the training? Why or why not?

In-Depth Response Questions

1. Do you think that Jami belongs in a **full-time special education classroom** setting for at least one school year to learn strong skills in assistive technology? If not, what placement option would you recommend? Explain your point of view with reference to policy, practice, and/or legislation. As per the Ministry of Education in Ontario (Ontario Ministry of Education, 2017), placement options to choose from are

    A *regular class with indirect support* where the student is placed in a regular class for the entire day, and the teacher receives specialized consultative services.

    A *regular class with resource assistance* where the student is placed in a regular class for most or all of the day and receives specialized instruction, individually or in a small group, within the regular classroom from a qualified special education teacher.

    A *regular class with withdrawal assistance* where the student is placed in a regular class and receives instruction outside the classroom, for less than 50 per cent of the school day, from a qualified special education teacher.

    A *special education class with partial integration* where the student is placed by the IPRC in a special education class in which the student–teacher ratio conforms to Regulation 298, section 31, for at least 50 per cent of the school day, but is integrated with a regular class for at least one instructional period daily.

    A *full-time special education class* where the student–teacher ratio conforms to Regulation 298, section 31, for the entire school day.

    Source: http://www.edu.gov.on.ca/eng/general/elemsec/speced/identifi.html

2. Following up from #1, investigate and explain what the role of the IPRC would be in making such a placement change.
3. Explain in detail how you think you could achieve better buy-in from Jami, if you were either one of his teachers or one of his parents.

4. Jami can invite a friend with him to this training. Comment on this unusual practice in terms of social–emotional–behavioural outcomes, inclusivity, **social justice**, and/or budget implications. Include recommendations as to how you would or would not change this program, and why.
5. Imagine that Jami's IEP team had suggested an alternative course for him in assistive technology skills. Use the below template to design his course, including at least three learning expectations for one term of study.

Special Education Program

To be completed for each subject/course with modified expectations and/or each alternative program with alternative expectations.

Student OEN/MIN:	Subject/Course/Alternative Program:

Current Level of Achievement: Pre-requisite course _____ Letter Grade/Mark _____ Curriculum Grade Level _____	Current Level of Achievement for Alternative Program:

Annual Program Goal(s): A goal statement describing what the student can reasonably be expected to accomplish by the end of the school year in a particular subject, course, or alternative program.

Learning Expectations (List modified/alternative expectations outlining knowledge and/or skills to be assessed, by reporting period. Identify grade level, where appropriate.)	Teaching Strategies (List only those that are particular to the student and specific to the learning expectations.)	Assessment Methods (Identify the assessment method to be used for each learning expectation.)

Figure 3.5.5 Alternative Course IEP Template

Source: Adapted from Ontario Ministry of Education, 2004. http://www.edu.gov.on.ca/eng/general/elemsec/speced/guide/resource/iepresguid.pdf, p. 54.

Suggested Resources

"Calming Source": Innisfil Boy Gets Help in School from Service Dog
http://barrie.ctvnews.ca/mobile/calming-source-innisfil-boy-gets-help-in-school-from-
service-dog-1.3162159

Center on Response to Intervention
http://www.rti4success.org/

Cystic Fibrosis in the Classroom
http://www.cfri.org/pdf/cfintheclassroom.pdf

Food Allergy Fact Sheet
http://www.nfsmi.org/documentlibraryfiles/PDF/20140912035026.pdf

Lions Foundation Canada Guide Dogs Promotional Video
https://www.youtube.com/watch?v=NBzaosI0vgk

Model Me Conversation Cues™—Video Modelling
https://www.youtube.com/watch?v=Bmz_c3z3JUI

My Stroke of Insight Ted Talk
http://www.ted.com/talks/jill_bolte_taylor_s_powerful_stroke_of_insight

National Service Dogs
http://www.nsd.on.ca/programs/certified-service-dogs-for-autism/

Read&Write for Google Chrome—Tutorial
https://www.youtube.com/watch?v=jhUXXBrXWOc

Right Hemisphere Brain Damage
http://www.asha.org/public/speech/disorders/RightBrainDamage.htm

Saskatchewan Brain Injury Association
http://www.sbia.ca/aboutbi.aspx

Service Dogs and Children with Autism Spectrum Disorders
http://aie.apsea.ca/images/info_papers/Service_Dogs.pdf

Service Dogs Policy
https://www.wcdsb.ca/ap_memos/PDF/APH020.pdf

References

Alzyoudi, M., Sartawi, A., & Almuhiri, O. (2015). The impact of video modelling on improving
social skills in children with autism. *British Journal of Special Education, 42*(1), 53–68.

American Academy of Sleep Medicine. (2001). *International classification of sleep disorders:
Diagnostic and coding manual.* Chicago, IL: American Academy of Sleep Medicine.

American College of Allergy, Asthma, & Immunology. (2014). *Anaphylaxis overview.*
http://acaai.org/allergies/anaphylaxis

American Speech–Language–Hearing Association. (2016). *FM systems.* http://www.asha.
org/public/hearing/FM-Systems/

American Speech–Language–Hearing Association. (2016). *Hearing assistive technology
(HATS) for children.* http://www.asha.org/public/hearing/Hearing-Assistive-
Technology-for-Children/

American Speech–Language–Hearing Association. (2016). *Right hemisphere brain damage.* http://www.asha.org/public/speech/disorders/RightBrainDamage.htm

Brain Injury Society of Toronto. (2016). *What is traumatic brain injury?* http://www.bist.ca/frequently-asked-questions-faq/#Q2

Burrows, K., Adams, C., & Spiers, J. (2008). Sentinels of safety: Service dogs ensure safety and enhance freedom and well-being for families with autistic children. *Qualitative Health Research, 18*(12), 1642–9.

Canada Revenue Agency. (2016). *Child disability tax credit.* http://www.cra-arc.gc.ca/bnfts/fq_cdb-eng.html#q1

Cystic Fibrosis Canada. (2016). *What is cystic fibrosis?* http://www.cysticfibrosis.ca/about-cf/what-is-cystic-fibrosis

Epilepsy Ontario. (2016). *What is epilepsy?* http://epilepsyontario.org/about-epilepsy/what-is-epilepsy/

GoQ Software. (2016). *wordQ.* http://www.goqsoftware.com/wordQ.php#!

Katayama, A. (2001). Bi-modal instructional practices in educational psychology: Mentoring and traditional instruction. *Journal of Instructional Psychology, 28*(3), 171–8.

Kern, L., & Clemens, N. (2007). Antecedent strategies to promote appropriate classroom behaviour. *Psychology in the Schools, 44*(1), 65–75.

Kurzweil Education. (2016). *How we help.* https://www.kurzweiledu.com/about-kurzweil/how-we-help.html

Levine, Z. (2010). Mild traumatic brain injury. Part 2: Concussion management. *Canadian Family Physician, 56*(7), 658–62.

Lundin, A., Boussard, C., Edman, G., & Borg, J. (2006). Symptoms and disability until 3 months after mild TBI. *Brain Inquiry, 20*(8), 799–806.

McIntosh, K., MacKay, L.D., Andreou, T., Brown, J.A., Mathews, J.A., Gietz, C., & Bennett, J.L. (2011). Response to intervention in Canada: Definitions, the evidence base, and future directions. *Canadian Journal of School Psychology, 26*(1), 18–43. doi:10.1177/0829573511400857

Mylan Specialty. (2016). *About EpiPen® (epinephrine injection) Auto-Injector.* https://www.epipen.com/en/about-epipen

(The) National Benefit Authority. (2016). *Disability benefits for scoliosis.* http://www.thenba.ca/disabilities/scoliosis/

National Institute of Health. (2016). Chronic pain: Symptoms, diagnosis, & treatment. *NIH Medline Plus, 6*(1), 5–6. https://medlineplus.gov/magazine/issues/spring11/articles/spring11pg5-6.html

National Institute on Deafness and Other Communication Disorders. (2016). *What is American Sign Language?* https://www.nidcd.nih.gov/

Ontario Ministry of Education. (2004). *The individual education plan: A resource guide.* Toronto, ON: Queen's Printer for Ontario. http://www.edu.gov.on.ca/eng/general/elemsec/speced/guide/resource/ipresguid.pdf

Ontario Ministry of Education. (2010). *Caring and safe schools.* http://www.edu.gov.on.ca/eng/general/elemsec/speced/Caring_Safe_School.pdf

Ontario Ministry of Education. (2013). *Learning for all: A guide to effective assessment and instruction for all students, kindergarten to grade 12.* http://www.edu.gov.on.ca/eng/general/elemsec/speced/LearningforAll2013.pdf

Ontario Ministry of Education. (2016). *Next steps: Provincial and demonstration schools.* http://www.edu.gov.on.ca/eng/parents/consult_pds.html

Ontario Ministry of Education. (2017). *The Identification, Placement, and Review Committee*. Toronto, ON: Queen's Printer for Ontario. http://www.edu.gov.on.ca/eng/general/elemsec/speced/identifi.html

Ontario Software Acquisition Program Advisory Committee. (2014). *Mandate*. https://www.osapac.ca/about-us/mandate/

Planas, N., & Civil, M. (2009). Working with mathematics teachers and immigrant students: An empowerment perspective. *Journal of Mathematics Teacher Education, 12*, 391–409.

Resiliency Initiatives. (2011). *Embracing a strengths-based perspective and practice in education*. http://www.mentalhealth4kids.ca/healthlibrary_docs/Strengths-BasedSchoolCultureAndPractice.pdf

Siddique, A., Abbas, A., Riaz, F., & Nazir, R. (2014). An investigation of perceptual learning style preferences of students on the basis of gender and academic achievements. *Pakistan Journal of Life and Social Sciences, 12*(1), 26–30.

Traumatic Brain Injury.com, LLC. (2001). *Mild TBI symptoms*. http://www.traumaticbraininjury.com/symptoms-of-tbi/mild-tbi-symptoms/

Tucker, B. (2012). The flipped classroom. *Education Next, 12*(1).

Turkstra, L., Politis, A., & Forsyth, R. (2015). Cognitive-communication disorders in children with traumatic brain injury. *Developmental Medicine and Child Neurology, 57*, 217–22.

Walia, H., & Mehra, R. (2016). Overview of common sleep disorders and intersection with dermatological conditions. *International Journal of Molecular Sciences, 17*(654), 1–11.

York Region. (2011). *Red flags: A quick reference guide for early years professionals in York Region*. https://www.york.ca/wps/wcm/connect/yorkpublic/054ca0a9-0027-46a3-b817-452890b3038b/red+flags+guide_web.pdf?MOD=AJPERES

Senior 4

Introduction

Chapter 4 is set around senior students in Ontario high schools (grades nine to 12), mostly in inclusive classrooms. Case 1 (Helmut) relates issues of a grade 11 student, Helmut. Helmut is a complicated teenager who is taking applied-level courses with an IEP for additional supports. His parents were newcomers to Canada, and encouraged Helmut to learn multiple languages. Helmut was diagnosed with Fetal Alcohol Effects at one point, but is now struggling with mental health issues and the justice system. Case 2 (High School with Trey) centres on Trey, a 16-year-old student with multiple diagnoses, who is living in foster care and supported by community agencies. Trey's IEP has accommodations, modifications, and alternative/locally developed courses, and he also has a safety plan. The current significant issue is the school's recommendation to move Trey to a segregated setting. Case 3 (Sharina, Self-Advocate) tells the story of Sharina from the point of view of Mr Savioni, a high school history teacher. Sharina is an English Language Learner as well as a student with a learning disability. Through the interaction between Sharina and her teacher, assistive technology is presented, as well as the tension between in-class accommodations, resistant teachers, and the need for effective self-advocacy. Case 4 (Kai's Blog) teaches through multiple blog entries written by Kai himself, a grade 12 student who is identified as gifted. This case presents a contrast between Kai's diagnosis, reporting, and IEP goal, and Kai's responses to the contents of those documents. Case 5 (Looking Back—Looking Ahead) traces the journey of an Ontario Certified Teacher through her school years as a student identified with Communication: Learning Disability at a young age. This culminating case presents lessons learned from that journey, as well as a full IEP.

Each case in Chapter 4 includes a range of brief response questions and in-depth response questions; resources, figures, and templates are included as needed. Integrated into each case are a range of keywords, which are defined in the margins, as well as in a glossary at the end of the book. Suggested readings, websites, articles, and multimedia are found at the end of the chapter, along with chapter references.

Case 1: Helmut

The head of special education read over the in-school team recommendations for Helmut, a grade 11 student in their large, busy, urban Catholic high school:

Helmut's placement will continue in inclusive classrooms at the **applied level**. His IEP development will continue with accommodations and some minor modifications to some of the subject areas—like last year.

The resource teacher will assist classroom teachers. Helmut will be timetabled into the resource room for work completion one period per day.

The school youth worker will see Helmut twice per week (whenever possible) to assist with problem behaviour, social judgment, and self-esteem-building activities. Helmut will continue to be encouraged to be involved in extra-curricular and community activities around his artistic and dramatic interests. A behaviour plan will be developed.

The **guidance counsellor** will continue to work with Helmut to help better prepare for post-secondary (**learning styles inventories, interest surveys**) to find motivators, and to seek out specialized programs and funding to share with Helmut's parents. The classroom teacher will confer with resource teacher and youth worker.

The in-school team will continue to monitor the effectiveness of the IEP. The resource teacher and homeroom classroom teacher will assist Helmut in preparation for the **Ontario Secondary School Literacy Test (OSSLT),** which has not yet been passed successfully (note: accommodations like visual supports for working memory and processing deficits will be required).

I am really sorry that I had to miss yesterday's meeting, reflected the head of special education. *Reading over this plan for Helmut's upcoming year with us, though, really impresses me! Although he is 16 now, he came to us as a seemingly very young—and what I thought was an immature—teenager. Although he remains one of our students of smaller stature, he has really risen high in so many ways. When he enrolled with us, he had just moved across the city to live with his aunt, and he was feeling pretty rough about himself. His parents had passed away years before in some sort of traumatic family incident—which is not discussed—but long before that, he had been accessing special education services.* "It looks like this started around grade two," *he commented aloud. He was already speaking German as well as English, as his family (including his aunt and now-deceased uncle) were newcomers to the country and the province. When we met together in grade nine, he told me that he had* "some problems." *He said his mom was drinking when was she was pregnant, and that he had what he called* "brain damage" *from all of this, but it wasn't his fault. The head of special education smiled when he recalled this, but became more sombre when he recalled discovering his diagnosis of*

Fetal Alcohol Effects. *Although he is a bit of what his teachers call "a loner," even now that he has been at the school for years and does have some close friends, he is really committed to our drama classes and the extra-curricular activities that come with it. He will do pretty much any tasks that have to do with theatre— though he refuses to act or sing—and everyone, including our staff, counts on him every term. He paints scenery, he creates backdrops, he gathers materials for props on the stage, he photocopies manuscripts, he video-records practices—it seems like a good match for his unending energy. And his ideas for our last post-apocalyptic landscape were amazing! He can't seem to stay on one task for more than maybe five minutes, but on the drama team, he just rotates from task to task and some- how it works just fine. We don't have to remind him all the time like we do in the classroom.*

The only glitch we had was when we changed the stage from a dump to a re- cycling centre, and he couldn't cope with this transition. He shouted a lot, stomped around the stage, and tore up some discarded materials, but calmed down pretty quickly. We don't even need a safety plan for him anymore. He has never been ag- gressive towards another person at school. His happy recollections broke when his extension rang in his office. He checked his cell phone for the time—*who could that be?* he wondered. *It's not even school time yet.*

"It's Helmut's aunt—remember me?" he heard, noting a disgruntled tone woven into her voice.

"Yes, of course I do," he responded, attempting to balance concern and warmth in his reply.

"I am going to get right to the point, here. And just so you aren't worried—I am not upset with the school. But I *am* upset with Helmut—and his so-called friends. To make a long story short—since I am guessing he hasn't told you himself—he was recently charged with breaking and entering after these 'friends' convinced him to enter a neighbour's home. Fortunately, or unfortunately, they had an alarm system, and the police were alerted. They found him in the living room, sitting with the homeowners' new puppy. So he appears in court next month, but our lawyer is hoping that the court will allow for a mental health diversion, which will help him to avoid a criminal conviction. What I am hoping from the school is some communica- tion (including paperwork) to the lawyer around any kind of mental health supports or diagnosis—anything—that you have in your files. Can you help?"

Ontario Secondary School Literacy Test (OSSLT) A province- wide test, which all students take at the same time near the end of the grade nine year, used to measure whether students are meeting the minimum standard for literacy at that grade level. Successful completion of the test is required to earn a diploma.

Fetal Alcohol Effects (FAE) A condition in which children exhibit one or more developmental and behavioural difficulties to varying degrees, such as hyperactivity, poor coordination, learning or language difficulties, or seizures, but not all the criteria for Fetal Alcohol Syndrome are met.

Brief Response Questions

1. What is your reaction to Helmut describing himself as "brain damaged"?
2. How could Helmut's difficulty with transitions be supported through his IEP?

continued

3. Should Helmut be taking the OSSLT? Why or why not?
4. When the head of special education further reviewed Helmut's OSR for more information, he found this assessment overview of his IEP, which was a quote from his medical assessment:

ASSESSMENT DATA

List relevant educational, medical/health (hearing, vision, physical, neurological), psychological, speech/language, occupational, physiotherapy, and behavioural assessments.

Information Source	Date	Summary of Results
Medical Assessment	Grade 4	Diagnosed with Fetal Alcohol Effects due to a smallish head, small, wide-set eyes, and high, pronounced cheekbones. Besides hyperactivity and learning challenges, Helmut appears to have poor judgment and can easily be led astray.

Figure 4.1.1 Assessment Information
Source: Adapted from Ontario Ministry of Education, 2004. http://www.edu.gov.on.ca/eng/general/elemsec/speced/guide/resource/iepresguid.pdf, p. 52.

Would this information be helpful for Helmut's aunt? Why or why not?
5. How could Helmut's areas of strength be integrated into his IEP and his program planning?
6. Will Helmut be awarded credits for his modified courses? Briefly explain with references to policy, practice, and/or legislation.
7. If Helmut had an identification, what would it likely be?

In-Depth Response Questions

1. How should the head of special education respond to Helmut's aunt? Why? Describe this in detail.
2. Using the *DSM-5* or a related publication, explore other labels or terminology related to prenatal alcohol exposure.
3. Helmut's Math course is an applied grade nine course with some minor modifications that are about two years below grade level. What would this course look like on his IEP? Use the below template and provide at least three to five goals for one term of instruction.

Special Education Program

To be completed for each subject/course with modified expectations and/or each alternative program with alternative expectations.

Student OEN/MIN:	Subject/Course/Alternative Program:

Current Level of Achievement:	Current Level of Achievement for Alternative Program:
Pre-requisite course _____	
Letter Grade/Mark _____	
Curriculum Grade Level _____	

Annual Program Goal(s): A goal statement describing what the student can reasonably be expected to accomplish by the end of the school year in a particular subject, course, or alternative program.

Learning Expectations	Teaching Strategies	Assessment Methods
(List modified/alternative expectations outlining knowledge and/or skills to be assessed, by reporting period. Identify grade level, where appropriate.)	(List only those that are particular to the student and specific to the learning expectations.)	(Identify the assessment method to be used for each learning expectation.)

Figure 4.1.2 Modified Program Template IEP

Source: Ontario Ministry of Education, 2004. http://www.edu.gov.on.ca/eng/general/elemsec/speced/guide/resource/iepresguid.pdf, p. 54. © Queen's Printer for Ontario, 2004. Reproduced with permission.

continued

Wechsler Intelligence Scale for Children (WISC) (Currently in version V) A psychological instrument used to measure intelligence in children. Structured in 16 subsets covering a range of areas, the WISC can help to identify specific learning or intellectual disabilities and strengths.

Verbal comprehension The ability to understand, analyze, interpret, and express oneself using written words.

Percentile A type of converted score that is expressed relative to a student's group in percentile points. It indicates the percentage of students tested who achieved scores equal to or lower than the specified score. 60th percentile means that 59 of 100 students in that same group scored lower than that child.

Perceptual reasoning The ability to interpret and learn from visual input; identify, analyze, and predict visual patterns; think about objects in three dimensions; and use visual information about objects and patterns to reason, extrapolate, and solve problems.

Working memory The part of short-term memory and other processing mechanisms used to plan and carry out behaviour, and to retain concepts and facts in the midst of action. It is used to stay focused on a task, and to recall information currently in use.

Processing speed A measure of the ability to automatically and fluently perform relatively easy mental calculations in a timely manner, without thinking them through.

Mental health diversion An option for an offender who has committed a minor criminal offence, and who has a mental health concern, in which the individual is required to seek mental health support in place of typical criminal justice consequences.

4. The psychoeducational report in Helmut's OSR gave some information about his WISC III: Verbal Comprehension—percentile indicates below average, Perceptual Reasoning—percentile indicates average, Working Memory—percentile indicates borderline, and Processing Speed—percentile indicates average. What accommodations might be necessary for this discrepancy in working memory? Discuss and make suggestions.

5. Access information about mental health diversion programs, and describe what might happen to Helmut if he is referred to one, in at least three paragraphs.

Case 2: High School with Trey

Trey didn't have an easy start to life, thought his current foster parent, one member of a couple who fostered two or three challenging teens every year. *I mean, he's a tall 16-year-old with a group of loyal friends at high school, now, but things haven't always been that way for him. He has been with me for most of his teen years, but he has never seen his birth father in that time—or any time since his apprehension by the Children's Aid Society. His birth mother was an addict when he was born and boasted about using street drugs when she was pregnant—at least that's what Trey was told. He has told me bits and pieces here and there, like that he has lived in so many foster-care placements that he has lost track, but that he likes how we live like a family here (even though the other two foster kids sometimes make him really angry), and that he hated being in a group home. It really seemed to make a difference for him when he started high school. There are so many other kids at our local high school that he was able to find a group of other grade 11s that he calls "my peeps." For whatever reason, he really identifies with them. They seem to put up with his issues—like that incessant skin-picking—and he seems incredibly supportive of them, telling me all the time about how what he called the "popular kids" are trying to get away with stuff behind the teachers' backs and how he stands up for his friends . . . which sometimes gets him into trouble, though. But maybe I should get to the task at hand—reviewing Trey's latest assessment results and school reports up until now—grade 11. It seems that there is some sort of issue around Trey's classroom for next year . . . his placement, I think the social workers called it. They said they want me to come to this year's IPRC with them; that there might be some big changes.*

She pulled the file folder given to her by the social workers at the Children's Aid Society (CAS), who act as Trey's legal guardians. CAS had written a summary of what they called "presenting concerns." She ran her eyes down this fairly lengthy list, eyes widening. *It's one thing living with these issues, but it seems different somehow—more painful—reading them on paper.* She read:

- Trey has had a long history of emotional and behavioural challenges since entering school, according to his OSR.
- Trey has poor impulse control and is easily frustrated with the smallest task at hand.
- Trey will act out with self-abusive behaviour: picking at his skin.
- Trey has a seizure disorder and is presently taking medication administered at home. Seizures are under control.
- Trey's present academic achievement in Language is at a low-grade-two level in all strands, and Mathematics is at a grade-three level in numeracy.
- Trey has been identified with a developmental disability.
- Trey has some speech problems (particularly with articulation) and tends to stutter when anxious.

Association for Community Living
An organization that supports individuals with intellectual disabilities through community participation. The organization provides leadership and engagement programs, organizes awareness campaigns, and supports research in promoting equality.

- Trey has an IEP in place with accommodations, modifications, alternative courses (including one in behaviour self-management), and locally developed courses.
- Trey has a safety plan in place.
- The in-school team at Trey's school is recommending a special class placement for all students with developmental disabilities (including Trey), and there is a class already established in the school.

First, she wondered: *What would this list look like if it included presenting strengths, like how the IEPs I have seen seem to balance that way? But, more importantly*—she started drumming her fingers on the table—*why on earth, exactly, would we pull Trey away from his friends for his last year of school? I know full well that CAS believes in inclusion, and if we want another voice, we could bring in the staff from the Association for Community Living with us to the meeting. We started meeting with them when Trey first came to us, and were told that he was identified at school with a developmental disability. One of the things they always emphasized to us was to fight for inclusion, and being at school with his neighbourhood peers, as well as the importance of community into adulthood beyond school. It seems to me that maybe this is one moment to do so—but I suspect we might see even more such moments as Trey moves into adult services.*

Non-credit (course)
Instruction on a set of skills that students may opt to take but which does not earn them credits towards completion of their Ontario Secondary School Diploma.

Ontario	Ministry of Education	**ONTARIO STUDENT TRANSCRIPT**			Date of Issue: 2016 06 30

Surname	Given names		OEN Number	Student Number	Gender
Boyned	Trey Allan		09876543BN	4343234	M

Name of District School Board	Number	Name of School	0	Number
Mansten District	06060	Sir Issac Newton Secondary		321

Date Month Year	Course Grade	Course Title	Course Code	Course Grade	Credit*	Notes
01/2016	11	Workplace Preparation	ENG3E	70	NA	IEP/MOD
01/2016	11	Healthy Living and Personal and Fitness Activities	PAF3O	67	1	IEP/ACC
01/2016	11	Drama Set and Design	ADS3O	88	NA	IEP/ALT
01/2016	11	Mathematic Skills for Entrepreneurs	MAT3O	75	NA	IEP/ALT
09/2015	11	Designing Your Future	GWL3O	72	NA	IEP/MOD
09/2015	11	Drama–Production	ADD3O	85	NA	IEP/ALT

*For students in any grade whose IEP describes modified curriculum expectations or alternative expectations that will not lead to a credit, enter NA in this column.

Figure 4.2.1 An Excerpt from Trey's Ontario Student Transcript

Source: Adapted from Ontario Student Transcript Manual, 2013. http://www.edu.gov.on.ca/eng/general/elemsec/ost/ost2013.pdf, p. 34.

She continued reading. This time, she looked back at his transcript, remembering all the creativity put into some of his **non-credit** high school courses so far. *I remember that it wasn't only kids like Trey who took these courses*, she recalled. *They were offered to anyone in the school! The classes weren't currently full, but nobody was excluded either. That's what I would call inclusion. Sometimes the school calls this reverse inclusion, but to me, it's just about providing ways for everyone to belong. The educational assistants in the classes then just helped anyone who needed help—they weren't "stuck to" any particular students. Trey used to tell me that nobody would talk to him when an EA was too close to him.*

Next in the file from CAS was entitled "In-School Team Recommendations." Trey's foster mom turned to that. *So, it looks like this is what the school is thinking that we should do next.* She read through, punctuating most of the points with comments (in her head):

(1) Continue monthly conference with Children's Aid guardian and Community Living representatives. *This makes good sense to me. I am really glad that the school sees the value in making sure everyone is on the same page and staying up to date on what is going on with Trey. But I think it's time for Trey to start attending the meetings. I think I read something about age 16 and meetings—I will have to see if I can find it.*

(2) Continue IEP development with a focus on locally developed courses in subject areas of interest to Trey. *I would say that I am a "yes" again for this one. These courses (and his friends) have stopped Trey from talking constantly about dropping out of high school. I believe he can go to school until he is 21. I think it's time to talk to Trey about this, as he is definitely thinking about next year as his last year. I find that it's a little disappointing that Trey isn't getting credits for his courses, though, since they are so valuable to him.*

(3) Continue peer–buddy strategies, EA support (at arm's length), and consultation with child and youth worker, Trey's doctor, the board's behaviour consultant, the SLP, CAS, and CMHA, as needed. *That's a lot of acronyms. And—a lot of support! I am not sure what the "peer–buddy" piece is related to, but I think Trey is okay in that area now.*

(4) Continue to advocate for a special class placement. *And there it is again. I think that it is time for me to teach Trey some more self-advocacy skills. At his age, it won't be just about me—or the CAS—advocating for inclusion. It will be about Trey himself being able to **self-advocate**. I wonder if there is a course in helping all of us to understand what he wants the most.*

Reverse inclusion Having students from other classrooms visit and participate in special education classrooms, with the goal of facilitating reciprocal friendships and fostering improved social skills.

Self-advocate (noun) Someone who seeks support or awareness for a particular cause that affects them personally, and who recommends a particular position or action on their own behalf; (verb) to speak up for one's own needs.

Belonging Feeling affinity for, and being welcomed and seen as, a member of a place or group.

Medical (needs) Physiological assessments—including vision, hearing, physical, diagnosis, or neurological—that provide information that might be helpful in understanding a student's characteristic requirements in the classroom.

Wechsler Individual Achievement Test (WIAT-III) A standardized academic achievement test used to measure knowledge in the areas of reading, written language, mathematics, and oral language.

Brief Response Questions

1. Find Ontario-specific information about age 16 and school-based special education meetings. Paraphrase your findings and include your source(s).
2. Find Ontario-specific information about age 21 and school services for students with exceptionalities. Paraphrase your findings and include your source(s).
3. What would the role of a behaviour consultant be in supporting Trey's education? Provide your ideas and refer to provincial, board, and/or school policy/policies.
4. What are your thoughts and/or experiences around non-credit courses in high school? Briefly describe at least two points.
5. Explain the difference between an alternative course in elementary grades and a locally developed course in high school.
6. Referring to the field of Applied Behaviour Analysis, what problem might exist with using a term like "acting out"? Reading about "operationalizing" problem behaviour might help.

In-Depth Response Questions

1. List, describe, and compare some benefits and detriments of inclusive placements versus specialized, segregated placements.
2. Why would the term "reverse inclusion" be used? Discuss this term, and compare it to both the terms "inclusion" and "belonging."
3. What are "peer–buddy strategies"? Define this term and add some similar terms and their meanings. Then, find at least two programs that utilize a peer–buddy–type strategy. Is this a practice you would use in your classroom and/or school? Why or why not?
4. How could Trey's self-advocacy skills be developed and supported in this situation?
5. Why is the foster parent not Trey's legal guardian? Discuss this in detail, including any potential impact that you might predict for parents and children in foster care (e.g., emotional).
6. The assessment component of Trey's IEP has a "**medical**" entry:

ASSESSMENT DATA
List relevant educational, medical/health (hearing, vision, physical, neurological), psychological, speech/language, occupational, physiotherapy, and behavioural assessments.

Information Source	Date	Summary of Results
Medical	Grade 9	• Trey has a seizure disorder and is presently taking valproic acid • Grand mal seizures are presently under control; petit mal seizures are observed at times especially if Trey is agitated or upset. • Ongoing logs of seizures are kept at home and school for the neurologist (seen every 4 months).

Figure 4.2.2 IEP Excerpt: Trey's Medical Information
Source: Adapted from Ontario Ministry of Education, 2004. http://www.edu.gov.on.ca/eng/general/elemsec/speced/guide/resource/iepresguid.pdf, p.52.

Explain how this information would help you, as well as any responsibilities you might have, as Trey's teacher, from this entry in his IEP.

7. The assessment component of Trey's IEP has four other entries: cognitive, speech–language, mental health, and academic:

ASSESSMENT DATA

List relevant educational, medical/health (hearing, vision, physical, neurological), psychological, speech/language, occupational, physiotherapy, and behavioural assessments.

Information Source	Date	Summary of Results
Cognitive WISC-V	Grade 10	• Results confirm Intellectual–Developmental Disability.
Speech–Language The CELF-5 (Clinical Evaluation of Language Fundamentals, 5th Edition)	Grade 10	• Indicates a significant delay.
The Structured Photographic Articulation Test—DII (SPAT-DII)		• Indicates a mild delay. (The SPAT-DII uses coloured photographs of a dog to illicit consonant sounds and determines phonological processes.)
The Structured Photographic Expressive Language Test		• Indicates a moderate delay.
The Goldman-Fristoe Test of Articulation-3 (GFTA-3)		• Age-appropriate sound errors.
Mental Health Re-assessment (through local Canadian Mental Health Association [CMHA])	Grade 10	• Re-assessment indicates that Trey continues to demonstrate high difficulties in unstructured environments. • Trey has high anxiety, depression, and an intellectual disability. • Trey continues to display self-injurious behaviour when anxious and/or frustrated.
Academic WIAT-III	Grade 10	• Overall behaviour profile is well below average. • Scores on the Anxious/Depressed, Social Problems, Attention Problems, Rule-breaking Behaviour, and Aggressive Behaviour scales are well below average. • Compared to same-age peers, the Adaptive Behaviour Composite is extremely low. *These results coincide with earlier assessments.

Figure 4.2.3: IEP Excerpt: Trey's Assessment Data

Source: Adapted from Ontario Ministry of Education, 2004. http://www.edu.gov.on.ca/eng/general/elemsec/speced/guide/resource/iepresguid.pdf, p.52.

As a classroom teacher, what information here will inform your teaching particularly well? Explain.

Case 3: Sharina, Self-Advocate

Guest Contributor: Adam Davies, BMus, MA, PhD student,
Ontario Institute for Studies in Education

English Language Learners (ELLs)
Students who are learning the English language at the same time that they are learning the curriculum being taught to them in English.

I am Mr Savioni, a high school History teacher at Summerside Secondary School. I have been teaching for 15 years—mostly History. I enjoy engaging with students on topics of North American history, world wars, human rights movements, and settler colonialism. As a teacher and as a human being, I am passionate about the various topics I teach, and I seek to engage with students while fostering their critical thinking. As passionate as I am about the material I teach, I am beginning to become frustrated with my students and with the varying needs that they present "these days" (a phrase I am often heard repeating). I find it exhausting providing accommodations to students and altering course materials to ensure the success of the various students with exceptionalities, and I do not appreciate the benefits of partaking in IEP meetings—No way!—nor discussing possible modifications to the curriculum.

Learning disability (LD)
An umbrella term for a wide variety of disabilities resulting from a number of neurodevelopmental disorders that affect the ability to acquire, retain, understand, organize, and/or use verbal and/or non-verbal information; may be associated with difficulties in social interaction; and are not the result of hearing/vision acuity, intellectual disabilities, socio-economic factors, cultural differences, language barriers, lack of effort, or education opportunities.

On Tuesday morning, I rushed into my classroom after having a whirlwind of a morning between rush-hour traffic and sleeping in. *I usually set my alarm, but I feel as though I purposefully forgot to set it in dread of waking up the next morning. With receiving administrative pressure to see higher scores in my classes, and my own feeling of frustration in a lack of student engagement in class, there seems to be an impossible amount of work to be done. Within my own grade 10 class, there are far too many students with individual needs, and I just do not have enough time to spend on ensuring all of them are successful!* As a History teacher, between grading essays and tests, I usually work with the resource teacher or special education specialists in my school to formulate accommodations for students, but all of this must be arranged in advance.

Just as the bell rang, I remembered that Sharina, one of my ELL students, also requires a piece of assistive technology, as she has a processing disability. *Rats! I forgot!* I thought with growing frustration. Sharina, an **English Language Learner (ELL)** in my grade 10 Canadian History class, has been in Canada for four years. Throughout her schooling experience in Canada, she has struggled not only due to being an ELL student, but also because she has a **learning disability (LD)**. After being recommended for testing in grade eight, Sharina discovered that she has a processing disability, which causes a delay in her ability to read text. According to the school psychologist, it was a really complicated assessment! Through the introduction of an Individual Education Plan, or IEP, with meetings following an Identification, Placement, and Review Committee, or IRPC, Sharina started to receive a plan that was individualized for her and provided her with the necessary curriculum accommodations to ensure her success. Usually, I arrange for a device to be used, such as **WordQ + SpeakQ**, which provides text-to-speech writing for students. I quickly reached for and scanned

WordQ + SpeakQ
Word-prediction software that supports literacy and writing through a variety of features. Word lists, text-to-speech, language dictionaries, thesaurus, and suggestions based on similar spelling and sounds allow the software to be adapted to suit individual needs. The SpeakQ plug-in allows for the software to provide speech-to-text, pronunciation, and reading feedback capabilities.

my notes, which confirmed that Sharina typically performs pretty well. *She will probably be fine just writing in class*, I thought to myself. *I have enough on my plate. I'll give her the test when she comes in with the other students and see how she does. I didn't even book time in the resource room! But wait . . . I thought. During a test earlier this year, I forgot to provide Sharina with an assistive device. I got in really hot water with our principal over that. Sharina stayed in for a bit of her lunch break to work through the test with me, but even with the one-to-one attention I gave her, her guardians still complained to the principal. Can you believe that?! Our principal, Ms Khan, informed me that I should have arranged for accommodations for Sharina by communicating with the special education department the day before the test. Which I didn't do this time. Again.* As the bell stopped ringing, the students filtered into the classroom.

They seem pretty happy today, I reflected. *Perhaps I'll be able to get through this and she will be just fine without her accommodations.* Everyone began to chat to one another and Sharina sat down with her friends at her usual seat at the back of the classroom. As the announcements began, I could tell that students were getting nervous.

Once the last speaker finished on the PA system, I picked up the pile of test papers and commenced handing them out. As I approached Sharina, I handed her the test, smiled, and continued walking about the classroom. I informed the class that they would have the full class period to write the test. Sharina quickly left her seat and approached me with her test folded up in her hand. Stating that she did not feel properly assisted to write the test, Sharina said that she would not write the test.

"I should not have to accommodate your needs . . . I have far too much to think about." I tried to put some bluster into my voice. *There. That should solve the problem. I told her that she could do it. She is okay. She'll be fine.* Sharina looked up at me with frustration.

"Mr Savioni," she said, "I am sorry, but you said that I would receive a piece of assistive technology during every assessment in class. This isn't fair." I thought about this, and then decided that Sharina was right. *There is really no way around this. She does deserve a fair assessment situation where she can achieve to the best of her ability.*

I sighed audibly. "Sharina, you are so right. I will call the special education department and see if Mrs Greensmith, one of our resource teachers, has a moment to set you up with a WordQ + SpeakQ program." I quickly used the classroom telephone while watching the remainder of the class write their test. After connecting with Mrs Greensmith, I sent Sharina down to the resource room with a copy of the assessment to work through it using WordQ + SpeakQ with Mrs Greensmith. *The resource teachers are so flexible*, I noticed. *Maybe I need to be more like them.*

The next morning, I returned to school and reflected upon the best way to assist Sharina in being successful in her schooling. *Well, although I have been stressed lately, that is no reason not to provide a student with everything possible to* be successful at school. As a teacher, I need to provide my students with what they need to show their learning, not hinder their ability to reach personal levels of success. I feel like I am a classic example, right now, of **resistance**. As I approached my desk, I noticed a sticky note on my desk:

Resistance A refusal to comply with or be affected by something. Can take the form of avoidance as well as active disagreement and opposition.

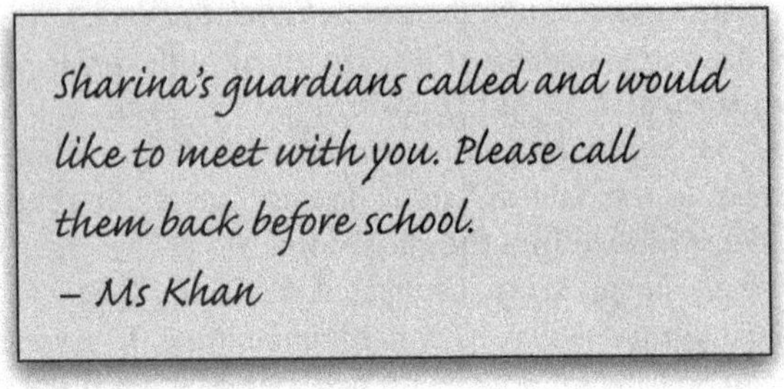

> Sharina's guardians called and would like to meet with you. Please call them back before school.
> – Ms Khan

Figure 4.3.1 Note from the Principal
Source: Author-generated.

I quickly went to the classroom phone, called Sharina's house, and made an appointment with her two guardians.

That afternoon, Sharina and her two guardians, Angela and Marina, walked into the classroom after school to meet with Principal Khan and me. As we sat down and welcomed them into the room, I became nervous, but I was confident that through a review of Sharina's previous schooling experience, various accommodations that have worked well for her, and some set goals for the future, we could all come up with a solution that would be best for Sharina.

After a detailed conversation, Sharina expressed that because she has difficulties with processing text and struggles with understanding concepts visually, she finds that text-to-audio devices, such as WordQ + SpeakQ, provide her with the ease to listen to what she has written to edit for errors and to hear the questions of the test spoken aloud to her through text-to-voice software. *Maybe it's not about me doing "favours," after all.* After a thorough review of Sharina's IEP, Ms Khan told Sharina and her guardians that she would receive the appropriate accommodations, as per her IEP. I could see Sharina's family starting to relax. I think they sensed that I was truly, finally, getting "on board." *Not a lot is different in this meeting compared to before . . . except me. Am I what everyone has been waiting for?* These accommodations would provide extra time on assignments, assistive technology—such as WordQ + SpeakQ—that could assist Sharina with processing text and editing her writing, as well as breaks when needed in testing situations. Further discussion around Sharina's comfort level in class occurred, and as everyone left the room, we all knew that we were working towards the same goal: Sharina's success at school. *I want Sharina to feel comfortable in class and not as though she is singled out,* I thought. *I really do care about her success—it's not about*

*her convenience. I should let her know how much I want to support her learning.
I will go home tonight and research other means of including her in class during testing situations that are **inclusive** and that keep her within our classroom community
during assessments.*

Inclusive Through
deliberately chosen
language and action,
ensuring that all students
can participate fully and
that nobody is excluded
or singled out.

Brief Response Questions

1. Why do you think that Sharina's classroom teacher was initially resistant to providing her documented accommodations?
2. Is it important that Sharina's teacher recognized this resistance? Why or why not?
3. How does the change of heart that Sharina's teacher has relate to the Standards of Practice and/or the Ethical Standards of the Ontario College of Teachers?
4. What does a "processing disability" mean?
5. What other type of assistive technology might help Sharina (e.g., Google Read&Write)?

In-Depth Response Questions

1. Using the below template, complete Sharina's list of accommodations in her IEP: environmental, instructional, and assessment.

ACCOMMODATIONS
(Accommodations are assumed to be the same for all subjects, unless otherwise indicated)

Instructional Accommodations	Environmental Accommodations	Assessment Accommodations

Figure 4.3.2 Sharina's IEP (Accommodations) Template
Source: Adapted from Ontario Ministry of Education, 2004. http://www.edu.gov.on.ca/eng/general/elemsec/speced/guide/resource/iepresguid.pdf, p.52.

continued

2.   Document the meeting with Sharina and her guardians, using the below template.

LOG OF PARENT/STUDENT CONSULTATION AND STAFF REVIEW/UPDATING

Date	Activity (Indicate parent/student consultation or staff review)	Outcome

Figure 4.3.3 Parent/Student Consultation Log
Source: Adapted from Ontario Ministry of Education, 2004. http://www.edu.gov.on.ca/eng/general/elemsec/speced/guide/resource/iepresguid.pdf, p. 56.

3.   How do you think that Sharina learned to be such a successful self-advocate? Provide a detailed response.
4.   Should Sharina write her tests using assistive technology in the inclusive classroom environment, or an alternate setting, such as the resource room? Why?
5.   Explain WordQ + SpeakQ in detail, with references to the software developer and the Ontario Software Acquisition Program Advisory Committee (OSAPAC) site.

Case 4: Kai's Blog

About Me

Hi—I'm Kai. I'm a 16-year-old student, still in high school, oppressed by my family (parents who are university professors—imagine), my school (they insist I have an "exceptionality"), my precarious employment (flipping burgers and making change), and my gender identity (questioning).

About This Blog

This blog is a place for writing about my problems. It's really a self-absorbed "all-about-me" kind of place where I can write about big ideas and rant about my life in a place where nobody knows my IRL identify—even though they will learn about the "real me."

Blog Entry #1: The Younger Me

When I was little, I went to this really weird private school—I think, anyhow. It was open-concept inside to support what they called child-led learning. In the middle of our "pods" of classrooms was sort of like a weight/cardio room, and around that was a set of "classrooms"—only they had no walls. So, when I was in grades four, five, and six (the "junior pod"), we could freely move between the different grades depending on our interests and motivation. Or so they told us! It's important that you know this about me: because of this system, I finished grades four to six in two school years in this set-up. Then seven and eight the year after that. I almost feel like I was doomed to be the "odd teen out" in the school where I am now—for many things about my not-quite-yet determined identity.

Blog Entry #2: What Happened Next

Once I finished grade 10, my parents wanted "to talk." You know that never leads to good things. This is when they really rocked my world—and not in a good way. My dad and my father said it was time for even better things to happen. Dad had found a new job, and they wanted a new life. The two of them packed up and moved us to the woods. And I mean literally the woods. No more after-school chemistry club; no more jazz band; no more anything I knew (or liked, really).

Blog Entry #3: High School or Home-School

So. School. Imagine what grade 11 was like. This little high school in this middle-of-nowhere town. My parents thought I was going to be able to go to the high school right near their university—that's what they were counting on in this move—but no freaking way that was happening! They fought forever, it seems like, in this up-tight little town, but the school boundaries were pretty solid, and there was no random private school around for me. So they told me this is it—it's either high school or home-school. Like I want to be home-schooled.

I headed off to the school, but I ended up just blending into the crowd. I found a few friends, sure, but nothing beyond that. We would probably fit the clichéd stereotype of high school just right. We eat lunch together. We sign up for classes together. Sometimes, we hang out after school together doing so-called nerdy things like coding and hacking that are kind of new to me—but way fun. I've never done anything so cool! But until one of us gets a licence ... it's kind of hard to get from place to place when there is what seems like a thousand kilometres between houses.

Blog Entry #4: Grade 12

Grade 12 is happening. I enrolled in all **academic courses** on track to university. Oh, but guess what else? That's right—I am "enrolled" in an IEP, as well. I can't just go and do my own thing—I have to have it documented on paper. They told me that I fit their "rules" for being exceptional, too, but that there really isn't any point in making it official at this point. Thankfully.

I have a little gift to share.

And you know how? That's right. The filing cabinet. Guess what I found? And guess what I did? That's right. I scanned it with my printer and put it right back. What is it? Well, apparently—it's me.

If you don't know what this means, this basically proves what I already know—I am smart and I like math and writing (as well as a bunch of other things that didn't make it to this list).

Academic courses
Course level that focuses on the fundamental principles of the discipline, explores related concepts, emphasizes theoretical and abstract applications of concepts, as well as incorporating practical applications. These courses are designed to prepare students for college and university courses after high school.

Cognitive (ability)
The constructs that allow individuals to acquire and retain knowledge, such as memory, organization, learning, understanding, reasoning, and attention.

ASSESSMENT DATA

List relevant educational, medical/health (hearing, vision, physical, neurological), psychological, speech/language, occupational, physiotherapy, and behavioural assessments.

Information Source	Date	Summary of Results
Cognitive Assessment—WISC-V (Full Scale)	*Grade 10*	*All sub-tests, reading comprehension and math problem solving plus sub-tests in verbal and perceptual reasoning, scored in the highly superior range.*
The Raven Standard Progressive Matrices (Raven SPM)		*Scored in the superior range.*
Curriculum-based assessments	*Grade 10*	*Reading comprehension and mathematics places Kai at a 2nd-year university level.*
		*Kai has high strengths in applied mathematics, writing, and reading according to **broad-based benchmark assessments**.*
		*Classroom-based **multiple intelligence** and **interest inventories** indicated superior engagement in applied mathematics and writing.*

Figure 4.4.1 Kai's Assessment Data from His IEP
Source: Adapted from Ontario Ministry of Education, 2004. http://www.edu.gov.on.ca/eng/general/elemsec/speced/guide/resource/iepresguid.pdf, p. 52.

Blog Entry #5: More about Me!

After all, blogs are all about being self-centred, aren't they?

So I was nosing around the house again. This time, I was checking in my parents' in-boxes. No, not the computer in-box (I don't go that far . . . yet). I mean the old-school ones on their desks. I found this lovely tome that apparently is a summary of me. I have retyped the pieces that I found particularly interesting.

Here are some:

In both grade 11 and 12 years, Kai was offered a range of programs that would accommodate for his exceptionality. An IEP is in place with accommodations to encourage greater peer involvement, leadership opportunities, plus extra-curricular activities.

Through a network of high schools across the county, we provide students with gifted exceptionality some **interdisciplinary** courses in **leadership** and character building, as well as co-op placements designed to foster **enrichment** activities. Kai has refused all of the classes and his parents support his decision. Kai's main focus is to excel at the top of his regular secondary academic classes.

Kai is a loner. He has no close friends among his peers. Students tend to ostracize him and have labelled him as a "nerd." Kai constantly worries about his grades and will become agitated if he does not achieve "perfection" on every task/assignment. The IEP team has met with his parents on two occasions. Kai's parents feel that the school and students are "picking on him" because he is intelligent and no one understands him. Apparently, Kai has no outside school interests. He spends all of his outside school time with his parents. Kai and his parents are ignoring everything that has been suggested in the IEP.

My response? Wait and see!

Blog Entry #6: So What?

I am definitely not a loner. I have a few friends, like I said. But my real community is online. At a runty little rural school with a small student body, it is not surprising to me that I can't find anybody who REALLY gets me. I have been told many times that this is sometimes easier at university when there is a huge number of people all co-existing together from all different places, BUT in the meantime, my friends are here, reading this. I can learn from reading e-books and watching YouTube videos, or—hello—from my dad. I don't need any sort of special "leadership" stream for that. I am just marking time here until I can get somewhere else.

I thought nobody could complain since (as I also read), "His assignments continue to be excellent." But apparently that's not good enough and I must also be depressed (though I can't argue with being called bored).

Apparently, also, I "refused to talk about the situation with the school youth counsellor." Or the guidance counsellor. That's right—I don't need everything I say

Raven Standard Progressive Matrices (Raven SPM) An assessment method designed to measure a student's ability to reason by analogy and form perceptual relations, without relying on knowledge of language or requiring any formal schooling.

Broad-based benchmark In Ontario, broad-based benchmark assessment is conducted province-wide, testing students' literacy and math skills to assist school boards in determining areas for growth in student achievement, teacher professional development, and needed resources. The test results are available to teachers, parents, students, and the public. The assessment is carried out at key stages of student learning by the Education Quality & Accountability Office (EQAO).

Multiple intelligences inventory An assessment method designed to measure a student's strengths and weaknesses in different intelligence areas in order to provide information on learning styles and capacities.

Interest inventory A method of assessment used to guide both teachers and students in forming a list of activities, subjects, and topics that a student enjoys. The student is asked a series of questions designed to help better understand themselves, their desires, their priorities, and their future goals.

to be pathologized and neuroticized by some stranger. And nobody else needs to label me a nerd. I label myself a nerd—nerds rule!

Some more snippets for you? Why yes! This is what they want me to do next.

> Kai will continue with IEP development with a focus on learning opportunities that encourage greater peer involvement, leadership opportunities, plus extra-curricular activities. (When are they going to realize that just because I am not following their pathway, doesn't mean there is a problem? I would actually GO if there happened to be something [anything?] interesting.)
>
> Kai will confer with school social worker who will make herself available to meet with and counsel Kai around his feelings. Father has given permission. (Ummmm . . . I guess they haven't tried foisting this particular professional on me yet. And just because I don't want to talk about my feelings doesn't mean they are a problem. THIS is where I talk about my feelings. If and when I want to do so. . . .)

See you tomorrow! Don't forget to follow my Instagram!

Interdisciplinary Addressing multiple content areas, or disciplines, in one unit or course.

Leadership The ability to effectively manage, inspire, and direct a group of people.

Enrichment Improving or enhancing the quality or value of education by going into the curriculum topics in more depth, making connections between sections of the curriculum, or learning beyond the curriculum.

Brief Response Questions

1. What is the typical identification marker for gifted exceptionality in Ontario school boards?
2. Where do you think the summary that Kai shared in Blog Entry #5 came from? Why do you think this?
3. It is sometimes said that IQ scores and the "gifted" label are biased towards children of educators. What is your response to this?
4. If you were a teacher at Kai's school and you happened to find Kai's blog, how would you react in your professional role? Link this to the Ontario College of Teachers' *Standards of Practice* and/or *Ethical Standards*.
5. In Blog Entry #4, Kai states that the school said, "but that there really isn't any point in making it official at this point" around his giftedness. Do you agree or disagree with this? Why?

In-Depth Response Questions

1. Why are gifted students often offered leadership training? Explain this, as well as an example of how such training might happen.
2. Do you think Kai's schooling (or its outcomes) would have changed if he had been identified as gifted very early in his school career? Why or why not? Explain and rationalize your point with reference to at least one related research study from a peer-reviewed source.

3. What do you think about Kai using a public blog space to work though his plans and emotions rather than meeting face to face will the school staff? Support your response in detail.

4. Access sample Ontario IEPs on the EduGAINS website (http://www.edugains.ca/newsite/SpecialEducation/transitions.html). Compare and contrast these IEPs with what you expect would be in Kai's IEP.

5. Freeman (2016) states that "Although electronic social media might have positive effects on learning, professional development, gifted advocacy, research, and policy-making, they might also encourage superficial rather than deep thought to negatively affect children's intellect and personal relationships" (p. 165). Read this article in its entirety and create a three-paragraph discussion around the information presented applied to Kai's case (see References for full bibliographic information).

Case 5: Looking Back—Looking Ahead

Communication: Learning Disability
One of the IPRC's subcategories, relating to a learning disability, that involves difficulty with receptive language, language processing, expressive language, or mathematical conditions. These usually result in a discrepancy between assessed intelligence and academic achievement.

Psychoeducational assessment
A measure of the academic and cognitive competencies of children, administered by a psychometrist, including memory, planning, organization, writing, mathematics, and reading. These assessments are used to guide instruction and involve gathering developmental, family, school, social/emotional, personality/temperament, and health histories.

Wechsler Intelligence Scale for Children (WISC) (Currently in version V) A psychological instrument used to measure intelligence in children. Structured in 16 subsets covering a range of areas, the WISC can help to identify specific learning or intellectual disabilities and strengths.

Intelligence The ability to acquire, understand, and apply knowledge and skills.

Verbal comprehension The ability to understand, analyze, interpret, and express oneself using written words.

My beginning in the teaching profession is atypical. Most of us start by choosing and doing—I began by overcoming. Through the process of becoming an Ontario Certified Teacher myself, I have had many chances to reflect on what happened to me along the way, and to think about how the special education processes did or did not work for me—and to figure out how to learn from those that did NOT. Ultimately, my story is a story of success—but not without struggle. As I leaf through the documents my parents collected throughout my childhood and into high school, I feel an overwhelming need to share my story—as an odd combination of hope and a warning of what not to do (at times).

It was only grade one when my six-year-old self was officially identified as **Communication: Learning Disability** through the IRPC's processes. This is very young to have such an identification. In fact, it's my understanding that most **psychoeducational assessments** aren't done for another few years, so I am not quite sure why mine happened when it did. Maybe my teacher could really see that I was struggling. The weird thing to me (obviously I didn't understand what was happening, then) from the point of view of a now-adult, is that my assessment didn't even ever explicitly diagnose me with a learning disability.

Back then, the gold standard tool for assessing intelligence was the **WISC-III**, which showed that I was supposed to have an IQ of 122. This is above average—but what is **intelligence** anyhow? Can it really be captured in a test like this? In any case, as I looked a little more at my assessment results, I see that the report said my **verbal comprehension** and my perceptual organization were average; that my visual perception and discrimination were borderline average; that my overall achievement in Language (reading and writing) were borderline average; and that my Mathematics (numeration) was low average. It seems that I also had a **central auditory processing** evaluation at the same time. So, overall, these tests also indicated a weakness with short-term memory, which is characterized by forgetting instructions, poor reading comprehension, and expressive language difficulties.

To get back to my point around the IPRC meeting, that's when it seemed that everything started happening. Knowing what I know now—that this committee *identifies* and *places* students with exceptionalities—I can see why things started changing afterwards. School sure wasn't the same for me—as a child. I didn't really know why, back then. I just knew that (for me) my friends were the best part of school, and then I wasn't allowed to be with my friends anymore. So instead of being in my school and my classroom in my own little neighbourhood, I was put on a school bus and taken every day to what they called (again, back then) a **"Learning Strategies"** class. Apparently this was targeted for students with learning disabilities. This went on for what seemed like forever to my primary student's mind . . . but really was until my grade four year. I remember then hearing the acronym "IEP" quite a bit, but not knowing what it meant. I did know, though, that it seemed to make everyone upset, and I got the feeling that I shouldn't talk about it. So it wasn't something I ever brought up—then.

My mom says by the time grade four came around they really had developed quite a stubborn streak and really pushed—what I would professionally (now) call "advocated"—for me to be back at my old school in the classroom with the kids who used to be my friends (called the "**regular**" **classroom**)—but who I hadn't seen all that much in the meantime. She says that by the time decision making came about at the IPRC meeting to prepare for my grade four year—they were ready. They had learned about LDs, education legislation, advocacy, and their rights. They always tell people at meetings that since I am their only child, they had lots of time and energy to devote to supporting me. They even brought an **advocate** with them to that meeting—a professor from a nearby university. In the end, I ended up right back where I started, but in grade four, of course.

It looks like one of the main problems with this transition is that quite a few of the teachers did not think I should be there, and they appeared to resist the accommodations suggested in my IEP (like assistive technology). But my dad said they really liked other parts—like sending me out for instruction in the resource room, and **modifying** my courses (Language and Math). He said they found the resistance part really hard: it seemed like the teachers thought that I couldn't learn.

But as my parents became advocates—so did I. My grade seven IEP included an **alternative course** in self-advocacy. A wonderful resource teacher taught me this course and she took her job with me very seriously. She somehow got me to move my thinking from, "I'm stupid!" to "I process information in a certain way—and this is it." Through this, I also learned that modifications have pretty serious implications once high school happens. I learned that course modifications may not be given credit, that students who have modifications are not usually recommended for academic courses, and then of course are not earning credits, which leads to problems around high school graduation, and all of this leads to difficulty getting into university. These weren't a big concern until I figured out that I want to be a teacher, and found out that teachers need two university degrees. That was it for me and modifications! I fought for grade-level courses with accommodations *ONLY*—and I learned that universities have accommodations, too.

I fought my way back from what my parents remember being called a "lag" of six to eight months throughout my junior and elementary years. By the time I was in grade nine, my Language skills were at an early grade eight level (whatever that means), and my Math skills were at late grade seven. One of my report card comments from the intermediate years said, "Trinity has worked hard on self-advocacy skills through her elementary years. She also struggled with organizational skills early on but has developed compensatory strategies."

In high school, my parents asked for the guidance counsellor head to summarize how I was doing. This is what they were given:

Trinity achieved an overall 78 and 79 per cent average in her grade nine and ten years at the "academic" grade level. No program modifications were given. Accommodations continued with resource assistance one period per day in the resource room.

Central auditory processing The part of the body that allows for the key auditory functions such as sound discrimination, pattern recognition, sound localization, and temporal masking.

Learning Strategies Practical plans of action to support academic success by ensuring students can obtain and retain information independently.

Intellectual disabilities An identification of an exceptionality as defined by the Ontario Ministry of Education in which the student's intelligence and information-processing speed is above the diagnostic category of mild mental retardation but below the low average range of intelligence.

Advocate Someone who seeks support or awareness for a particular cause, and who recommends a particular position or action on someone else's behalf.

Regular classroom Conventional classroom that all students not assigned to an alternative classroom or school attend, averaging 20–30 students with a variety of abilities and learning needs in each, and organized by grade.

Modified course
A subject or course with changes made to the age-appropriate grade-level expectations in order to meet a student's learning needs. These changes may involve using expectations developed for a different grade level and/or increasing or decreasing the number and/or complexity of the regular-grade-level curriculum expectations.

Alternative course
Subjects developed on a student's IEP to address various aspects of student need that are not specifically represented in the Ontario curriculum, so the student can learn new skills. These may include areas such as social skills, communication skills, or money management, depending on individual need. At the high school level, these would not be given formal credits.

Learning Strategies credit Courses in grades nine and 10 that focus on providing practical plans of action to support academic success by ensuring students can obtain and retain information independently.

Instructional accommodations—assistive technology, verbal cues, board notes, extra time as required to complete tasks, note-taking assistance, class buddy, repetition of instructions, visual cueing plus word retrieval prompts.

Environmental accommodations—alternative work space and/or strategic seating as required, minimal background noise.

Assessment accommodations—alternative setting, assistive technology, extended time, frequent breaks, oral responses (audio recording if possible), prompts for on-task behaviour.

It's at this point—I remember—that we all really thought that maybe, just maybe, I could do this! Everyone started pulling together with us, too. An updated psychoeducational assessment was arranged—well, advocated for (and paid for)—and this happened while I was in grade 11.

CONFIDENTIAL: PSYCHOEDUCATIONAL REPORT

Student Information

Gender:	Female—Trinity
DOB:	16 August
Current Age:	17 years
Family Demographics:	Living with both parents. Trinity is an only child.
School:	Large urban secondary school
Current grade/placement:	Grade 11 Academic
Identification: Communication:	Learning Disability (most recent IPRC 19 May)

Presenting Concerns:
Parents have expressed some concern that school communication with parents and Trinity around IEP development and her achievement has not been consistent in the past (beyond the reporting times). Trinity and parents have asked that at least two meetings be arranged each semester for parents and Trinity to meet with her subject teachers and the resource teacher. Trinity has expressed concern that her time in the resource room, although highly productive, has not been fully recognized for a **Learning Strategies credit**.

IEP accommodations are not always emphasized in each subject class. All subject teachers need to be fully aware of the IEP accommodations and consistent in application.

Assessment (at 16 years, 10 months)
Reason for referral: Trinity was referred by the secondary in-school team to update an assessment given in her grade one year. Trinity is entering her senior secondary years. Trinity hopes to attend a local university to eventually earn her teacher certification.

Cognitive: A WISC-V was administered. The Full Scale included sub-tests in reading comprehension/writing and math problem solving plus sub-tests in verbal and perceptual reasoning. The overall results indicated an above-average intelligence quotient of 125. Trinity's testing in vocabulary, associative thinking, and long-term memory was in the "Low Average" range. Her ability to infer and define relationships fell in the average range. A **Wide Range Assessment of Memory and Learning–Second Edition (WRAML-2)** was administered. Trinity fell in the "Average" range. Perceptual reasoning score also fell in the "Average" range. **Executive functioning** skills were assessed. Trinity's score fell below the **1st percentile**, which indicates difficulties in task behaviour/task completion. Trinity's processing speed and **motor integration** were both "above average." Trinity should have no difficulty scanning for contextual cues, copying notes, and recording.

Academic Achievement: A WIAT-II was administered. Reading, spelling, and decoding were at a grade seven equivalent; written expression was at a grade 12 equivalent. Mathematics testing indicated a grade level of six in both numeration and problem solving.

In-School Team Recommendations
Recommendations made to the in-school team include:

- Continue with IEP development and accommodations in place. Greater emphasis around accommodation strategies should increase organizational skills. Use of WordQ assistive technology to assist Trinity's spelling and Kurzweil to assist "processing" in reading comprehension/sight word vocabulary/word identification/rate. Trinity has difficulties retaining information in short-term memory. It is important to apply assistive technology to increase listening with meaning. Also, requesting verbal feedback will assist listening skills and help to clarify. Develop vocabulary through categorization, association, and classification.
- In Trinity's assessment allow for oral testing plus multiple-choice-style questioning. Trinity does have significant difficulties in Mathematics and will struggle in any secondary Math class without program modifications.
- Continue with one period per day in the learning resource room for assistance in completion of subject class assignments (subject teachers to give non-verbal cues including praise for staying on task). Trinity is to be supplied with school laptop for class and home. Trinity is a very hard-working student who should be highly commended and encouraged for her work ethic.
- With the resource teacher's assistance, work with Trinity to approach the principal around credit recognition for her hard work in the resource room.
- All subject teachers need to be consistent in the application of Trinity's accommodations required as stated in her IEP.
- Continue regular contact/achievement updates with parents and Trinity.
- Encourage Trinity to partake in her transition planning for post-secondary schooling.

Wide Range Assessment of Memory and Learning (WRAML-2) An assessment that helps to determine the student's working memory capacity. It evaluates both short- and long-term memory as well as cognition (i.e., the ability to learn new material).

Executive functioning Higher-order thinking processes involved in coordinating and controlling other cognitive abilities and behaviours. They include both organizational and regulatory functions such as planning, self-control, working memory, decision making, and abstract thinking.

1st percentile The 1st percentile represents the lowest percentile score (i.e., lowest score relative to the student's peer group), indicating a great deal of difficulty in the task being performed.

Motor integration Output of physical movement in response to input from another sensory source (e.g., visual, auditory).

Figure 4.5.1 Trinity's Psychoeducational Assessment Report Excerpt
Source: Author-created.

Individual Education Plan

REASON FOR DEVELOPING THE IEP

☒ Student identified as exceptional by IPRC   ☐ Student not formally identified but requires special education program/services, including modified/alternative learning expectations and/or accommodations

STUDENT PROFILE

Name: _Trinity Smith_   Gender: _F_   Date of Birth: _26/2_

School: _Furrowdale Secondary School_

Student OEN/MIN: _89674523_   Principal: _Paul Dosser_

Current Grade/Special Class: _11_   School Year: _____

Most Recent IPRC Date: _June_   Date Annual Review Waived by Parent/Guardian: _____

Exceptionality: _Communication: Learning Disability_

IPRC Placement Decision (check one)
☒ Regular class with indirect support
☐ Regular class with resource assistance
☐ Regular class with withdrawal assistance
☐ Special education class with partial integration
☐ Special education class full-time

ASSESSMENT DATA

List relevant educational, medical/health (hearing, vision, physical, neurological), psychological, speech/language, occupational, physiotherapy, and behavioural assessments.

Information Source	Date	Summary of Results
Speech–Language Assessment	Grade 2	Significant delays in the areas of expressive language, auditory memory, and sound awareness. Mild delay in the area of receptive language.
Hearing/Central Auditory Processing Assessment	Grade 2	Auditory integration weakness and significant difficulty with sound blending.
Psychological Assessment	Grade 1	Showed a wide variation in learning abilities. Trinity demonstrates a strength in processing speed. Trinity demonstrates weaknesses in executive functioning skills, especially in the area of working memory.

STUDENT'S STRENGTHS AND NEEDS

Areas of Strength	Areas of Need
Perceptual organization	Auditory integration
Processing speed	Executive function
Verbal comprehension	Expressive language
Work effort	Receptive language
	Short-term auditory and visual memory

SUBJECTS, COURSES, OR ALTERNATIVE PROGRAMS TO WHICH THE IEP APPLIES

Identify each as Modified (MOD), Accommodated only (AC), or Alternative (ALT)

SEMESTER ONE

1. ENG3U (English) — ☐ MOD ☒ AC ☐ ALT
2. ADA3M (Drama) — ☐ MOD ☒ AC ☐ ALT
3. Work Placement — ☐ MOD ☒ AC ☐ ALT
4. Work Placement — ☐ MOD ☒ AC ☐ ALT

SEMESTER TWO

1. FSF3U (French) — ☐ MOD ☒ AC ☐ ALT
2. GPP3O (Leadership) — ☐ MOD ☒ AC ☐ ALT
3. MCR3U (Math) — ☐ MOD ☒ AC ☐ ALT
4. SBI3U (Biology) — ☐ MOD ☒ AC ☐ ALT

Elementary Program Exemptions or Secondary School Compulsory Course Substitutions

☐ Yes (provide educational rationale)   ☒ No

Complete for secondary students only:

Student is currently working towards attainment of the:

☒ Ontario Secondary School Diploma   ☐ Ontario Secondary School Certificate   ☐ Certificate of Accomplishment

ACCOMMODATIONS

(Accommodations are assumed to be the same for all subjects, unless otherwise indicated)

Instructional Accommodations	Environmental Accommodations	Assessment Accommodations
Verbal cues for transitions Read-aloud board notes Provide class notes ahead of time Conference with student regarding oral reading Allow extra time for processing Provide high-structure activities Use partnering and small-group work Repetition of information Reword and rephrase often Use visual cues Use word-retrieval prompts Use laptop and software for note taking and assignments	Alternate work space Preferential seating (near instructor) Minimize background noise FM system use in class	Use of computer for test taking Provide clarification of questions and instructions Alternative settings Extra time Prompts for returning to task

Individualized Equipment   ☒ Yes (list below)   ☐ No

Laptop

continued

LOG OF PARENT/STUDENT CONSULTATION AND STAFF REVIEW/UPDATING

Date	Activity (Indicate parent/student consultation or staff review)	Outcome
30 August	Meeting with parents and Trinity to discuss IEP goals and courses for this school year.	Trinity will take university English in the same term as her work placement so she can focus more time on English.
19 Sept	IEP sent home to be signed by Trinity and her parents.	IEP returned signed.

The principal is legally required to ensure that the IEP is properly implemented and monitored.

This IEP has been developed according to the ministry's standards and appropriately addresses the student's strengths and needs. The learning expectations will be reviewed and the student's achievement evaluated at least once every reporting period.

P. Dosser   _15 Sept_

Principal's Signature   **Date**

Involvement of Parent/Guardian and Student (if student is 16 or older)

	Parent/Guardian	Student
I was consulted in the development of this IEP	☒ Parent/Guardian	☒ Student
I declined the opportunity to be consulted in the development of this IEP	☐ Parent/Guardian	☐ Student
I have received a copy of this IEP	☒ Parent/Guardian	☒ Student

Parent/Guardian and Student Comments:

M. Smith   _19 Sept_

Parent/Guardian Signature   Date

Trinity Smith   _19 Sept_

Student Signature (if 16 or older)   Date

Transition Plan

Student's name: _Trinity Smith_   **OEN/MIN:** _89674523_

Specific Goal(s) for Transition to Post-secondary Activities

Trinity will complete a Work Placement (Co-op) in an ELKP classroom at her previous elementary school.

Trinity will explore university options by attending the career fair in October.

Actions Required	Person Responsible for Actions	Timelines
1. Consult with placement teacher regarding Trinity's IEP.	1. Resource Teacher	1. 3 Sept.
2. Ensure Trinity has access to attend the career fair in October.	2. Resource Teacher	2. 24 Oct.

Figure 4.5.2 Trinity's Grade 11 IEP

Source: Adapted from Ontario Ministry of Education, 2004. http://www.edu.gov.on.ca/eng/general/elemsec/speced/guide/resource/iepresguid.pdf

So there is not much to tell from this point—grade 11—in high school. I struggled, but persevered, and experienced a great deal of support. I graduated with my OSSD. I completed a BA, a BEd, and filled out my application to be certified as a professional teacher in the province of Ontario. And now? Well, one thing that I noticed in my program of teacher certification was that I had many peers who loved—really loved—school. I wasn't like that. But many of our students aren't like that, either. I think it's great for our schools to have educators who know, first-hand, what it's like to struggle, to push, and to succeed through hardship—it has a different flavour than just being good at school. Now I am working my way through Additional Qualifications courses (while I teach a variety of primary/elementary grades in a variety of roles) to become a special educational specialist, and—one day—a resource teacher who can empathize, support, and advocate, and change the pathways of the lives I encounter along the way.

Ontario Secondary School Diploma (OSSD) Certification of high school completion in Ontario. The diploma indicates completion of 18 compulsory credits, 12 elective credits, provincial literacy requirement, and 40 hours of community involvement.

Brief Response Questions

1. What is a "grade-level" or an "age-level equivalent"? Define one or both of these terms.
2. Find some costs of private psychoeducational assessment in your area and give two points about why parents might pursue these, as well as two points about why they might not.

continued

3. Do you think a video like "What are LDs?" would have helped Trinity? Why or why not?
4. Do you feel that more time should have been spent teaching Trinity related skills in assistive technology? If so, provide at least one example. If not, why not?
5. What is one other step you would include in Trinity's transition plan? Include the person responsible for this step, and its timeline within the school year.

In-Depth Response Questions

1. Neither of Trinity's psychoeducational assessments resulted in a diagnosis of an LD. However, she was identified as a student with a Communication: LD through the school system. How is this possible? Explain in detail, referencing legislation, policy, and/or practice.
2. Trinity has a psychoeducational assessment update scheduled in grade 11. Why would this be necessary or desirable?
3. Trinity had psychoeducational assessments in grade one and in grade 11. Why would such a lengthy gap exist between assessments? Is this common practice in Ontario schools? Explain.
4. It appears that some of Trinity's teachers were resistant to following her IEP. Explain the responsibilities of teachers to implement IEPs, referencing legislation and/or policy around Ontario special education practices.
5. Read "York University Student Wins Mental-Health Fight" (Zlomislic, 2016; see below for full reference information). Do you think this could change a case like Trinity's? If not, why not? If so, how could it change the case?
6. Review "Educational Implications of Recent Supreme Court Ruling" (Learning Disabilities Association of Ontario, 2015; see below for full reference information). Do you think this could change a situation like Trinity's? If not, why not? If so, how could it change the case?

Suggested Resources

Developing Effective IEPs
https://www.youtube.com/watch?v=Zf7H6NHoWpU

EduBlogs by Ontario Teachers (TeachOntario/TVO, n.d.)
https://www.teachontario.ca/community/explore/teacher-blogs

Educational Implications of Supreme Court Ruling on Moore Case
http://www.ldao.ca/educational-implications-of-recent-supreme-court-ruling/

EduGAINS Sample IEPs
http://www.edugains.ca/newsite/SpecialEducation/transitions.html

Fetal Alcohol Exposure
http://pubs.niaaa.nih.gov/publications/FASDFactsheet/FASD.pdf

Giving & Getting: Using Social Media for Professional Online Collaboration
http://www.cea-ace.ca/education-canada/article/giving-and-getting

Guide to Locally Developed Courses, Grades 9–12
http://www.edu.gov.on.ca/eng/document/curricul/secondary/localdev/locdeve.pdf

Law Facts: Mental Health Court
http://lawfacts.ca/mental-health/court

Mental Health Diversion and Court Support
http://ontario.cmha.ca/mental-health/services-and-support/justice-services/
    mental-health-diversion-and-court-support/

Ontario College of Teachers: Ethical Standards
http://www.oct.ca/public/professional-standards/ethical-standards

Ontario College of Teachers: Standards of Practice
http://www.oct.ca/public/professional-standards/standards-of-practice

Ontario Special Needs Roadmaps for School
https://www.youtube.com/watch?v=Zf7H6NHoWpU

Possible Effects of Electronic Social Media on Gifted and Talented Children's Intelligence and Emotional Development
http://gei.sagepub.com/content/32/2/165.full.pdf+html

(The) Psychological Well-Being of Early Identified Gifted Children
http://gcq.sagepub.com/content/60/1/16.full.pdf+html

Students Use Social Media to Improve Mental Health on Campus
http://www.camh.ca/en/hospital/about_camh/newsroom/news_releases_media_
    advisories_and_backgrounders/current_year/Pages/Students-use-social-media-to-
    improve-mental-health-on-campus.aspx

What Are Learning Disabilities?
https://www.youtube.com/watch?v=wCqeFxDgacQ

References

American Speech-Language-Hearing Association. (2016). *Knowledge and skills needed by speech-language pathologists with respect to reading and writing in children and adolescents.* http://www.asha.org/policy/KS2002-00082/

Banting Memorial High School. (n.d.). *Perceptual reasoning index.* http://ban.scdsb.on.ca/Documents/SpecEd_PercepIndex.pdf

Bauer, G. (2005, March). Teaching the gifted. *Professionally Speaking.* http://professionallyspeaking.oct.ca/march_2012/features/teaching_the_gifted.aspx

Bennett, S., Dworet, D., & Weber, K. (2013). *Special education in Ontario schools* (7th ed.). St Davids, ON: Highland Press.

Canadian Association for Community Living. (2016). *About us: Our mission statement.* http://www.cacl.ca/about-us

Canadian Mental Health Association: Ontario. (2016). *Mental health diversion and course support.* http://ontario.cmha.ca/mental-health/services-and-support/justice-services/mental-health-diversion-and-court-support/

Canivez, G., Watkins, M., & Dombrowski, S. (2016). Factor structure of the Wechsler Intelligence Scale for Children–Fifth Edition: Exploratory factor analysis with the 16 primary and secondary subtests. *Psychological Assessment, 28*(8), 975–86.

Career Cruising. (2015). *St Thomas Aquinas Catholic Secondary School: Guidance and career education.* https://www.careercruising.com/Individual/CP_CourseCalendar.aspx?SID=8448&DID=14745

Cram, H., Krupa, T., Missiuna, C., Lysaght, R., & Parker, K. (2016). The expanding relevance of executive functioning in occupational therapy: Is it on your radar? *Australian Occupational Journal, 63,* 214–17.

de la Guia, D., Lozano, M., & Penichet, V. (2015). Educational games based on distributed and tangible user interfaces to stimulate cognitive abilities in children with ADHD. *British Journal of Educational Technology, 46*(3), 664–78.

District School Board of Niagara. (2016). *Academic pathways.* http://www.dsbn.org/studentsuccess/index.aspx?id=13546

Doucette, M., Kurth, S., Chevalier, N., Munakata, Y., & LeBourgeois, M. (2015). Topography of slow sigma power during sleep is associated with processing speed in preschool children. *Brain Science, 5*(4), 494–508.

Education Quality and Accountability Office. (2015). *Ontario secondary school literacy test.* http://www.eqao.com/en/assessments/OSSLT

Frawley, P., & Bigby, C. (2015). Reflections on being a first generation self-advocate: Belonging, social connections, and doing things that matter. *Journal of Intellectual and Developmental Disabilities, 40*(3), 254–64.

Freeman, J. (2016). Possible effects of electronic social media on gifted and talented children's intelligence and emotional development. *Gifted Education International, 32*(2), 165. doi:10.1177/0261429414557591

GoQ Software. (2016). *wordQ+speakQ.* http://www.goqsoftware.com/wordQspeakQ.php

Heine, C., & O'Halloran, R. (2015). Central Auditory Processing Disorder: A systematic search and evaluation of clinical practice guidelines. *Journal of Evaluation in Clinical Practise, 21,* 988–94.

Huntsman, C. (n.d.). *Using and understanding test scores.* University of Nevada, Las Vegas. https://faculty.unlv.edu/daniello/usingandunderstandingtestscores.pdf

Kaufman, A., & Lichtenberger, E. (2000). *Essentials of WISC-III and WPPSI-R assessment.* Hoboken, NJ: John Wiley & Sons Inc.

Lange, R. (2011). Verbal comprehension index. In J. Kreutzer, J. DeLuca, & B. Caplan (Eds.), *Encyclopedia of clinical neuropsychology* (pp. 2602–3). New York, NY: Springer.

Learning Disabilities Association of Ontario. (2015). *Official definition of LDs.* http://www.ldao.ca/introduction-to-ldsadhd/what-are-lds/official-definition-of-lds/

Mack, F. (1996). Parent knowledge of Fetal Alcohol Syndrome and Fetal Alcohol Effects: Michigan survey. Presented at the Michigan Federated Chapters of The Council for Exceptional Children Convention. Grand Rapids, Michigan.

Mainwaring, D. (2015). Creating a safe space: A case study of complex trauma and a call for proactive comprehensive psychoeducational assessments and reviews. *Journal of Psychologists and Counsellors in Schools, 25*(1), 87–103.

Messer, D., Henry, L., & Nash, G. (2016). The relation between executive functioning, reaction time, naming speed, and single word reading in children with typical development and language impairments. *British Journal of Educational Psychology, 86,* 412–28.

Nicola, K., & Watter, P. (2016). Visual–motor integration performance in children with severe specific language impairment. *Child: Care, Health and Development, 42*(5), 742–9.

Ontario Institute for Studies in Education. (2016). *Communication exceptionalities: Learning disability*. http://www.oise.utoronto.ca/adaptivetech/Special_Ed/Communication_Exceptionality/Learning_Disability/index.html

Ontario Ministry of Education. (2000). *Ontario student record (OSR) guideline*. http://www.edu.gov.on.ca/eng/curriculum/secondary/altCredit_Different.html

Ontario Ministry of Education. (2004). *The individual education plan: A resourceguide*. Toronto, ON: Queen's Printer for Ontario. http://www.edu.gov.on.ca/eng/general/elemsec/speced/guide/resource/ipresguid.pdf

Ontario Ministry of Education. (2006). *Guidance and career education*. http://www.edu.gov.on.ca/eng/curriculum/secondary/guidance910currb.pdf

Ontario Ministry of Education. (2008). *Supporting English Language Learners: A practical guide for Ontario educators*. http://www.edu.gov.on.ca/eng/document/esleldprograms/guide.pdf

Ontario Ministry of Education. (2013). *The Ontario Student Transcript (OST) manual*. http://www.edu.gov.on.ca/eng/general/elemsec/ost/ost2013.pdf

Ontario Ministry of Education. (2014). *Identification of and program planning for students with learning disabilities. Policy/program memorandum no. 8*. http://www.edu.gov.on.ca/extra/eng/ppm/ppm8.pdf

Ontario Ministry of Education. (2016). *What do you need to graduate?* http://www.edu.gov.on.ca/extra/eng/ppm/graduate.html

Ontario School Counsellors' Association. (2015). *The role of guidance teacher–counsellor*. https://www.osca.ca/images/Role_of_Counsellor.pdf

Pearson. (2016). *WISC-V: Discover the power of V*. http://www.wiscv.com/

Pearson Clinical. (2016). *Wide range assessment of memory and learning, second edition*. https://www.pearsonclinical.ca/en/products/product-master/item-108.html

Perez, K., & Salgado, M. (2016). Same plans, different strategies: The multiple faces of resistance. *Pedagogy, culture, & society, 24*(4), 617–30.

Polly, D., & Rock, T. (2016). Elementary education teacher candidates' integration of technology in the design of interdisciplinary units. *Tech Trends, 60*, 336–43.

Psych-Ed. (n.d.). *What is a psycho-educational assessment?* http://www.psych-ed.ca/index.html

Ruiz-Gallardo, J., Lopez-Cirugeda, I., & Moreno-Rubio, C. (2012). Influence of cooperative learning on students' self-perception on leadership skills: A case study in science education. *Higher Education Studies, 2*(4), 40–8.

Schoger, K. (2006). Reverse inclusion: Providing peer social interaction opportunities to students placed in self-contained special education classrooms. *TEACHING Exceptional Children Plus, 2*(6), 1–11.

Slack, N., & Norwich, B. (2007). Evaluating the reliability and validity of a learning styles inventory: A classroom-based study. *Educational Research, 49*(1), 51–63.

Taormina, R., & Gao, J. (2013). Maslow and the motivation hierarchy: Measuring satisfaction of the needs. *The American Journal of Psychology, 126*(2), 155–77.

VanTassel-Baska, J., & Stambaugh, T. (2005). Challenges and possibilities for serving gifted learners in the regular classroom. *Theory into Practise, 44*(3), 211–17.

Zlomislic, D. (2016, 12 January). York University student wins mental-health fight. *Toronto Star*. https://www.thestar.com/news/gta/2016/01/12/york-university-student-wins-mental-health-fight.html

Zytowski, D. (1998). Ellenore Flood's Kuder Occupational Interest Survey and Career Search Schedule. *Career Development Quarterly, 46*(4), 320–9.

Glossary

Academic courses Course level that focuses on the fundamental principles of the discipline, explores related concepts, emphasizes theoretical and abstract applications of concepts, and incorporates practical applications. These courses are designed to prepare students for college and university courses after high school.

Accommodative esotropia Crossed eyes caused by the extra focusing efforts (called accommodation) of the eyes as they try to see clearly, typically resulting from eyes that are farsighted (hyperopic). A side effect of the accommodative effort can be excess convergence or crossing of the eyes. If a child's eyes cross at an early age, then vision may not develop normally and may be permanently reduced in one eye.

Advocate Someone who seeks support or awareness for a particular cause, and who recommends a position or action on someone else's behalf.

Allergy An immune response by the body to a substance to which the body is hypersensitive. Reaction severity can range from mild swelling or difficulty breathing to vomiting, pain, asphyxiation, and death.

Alternative courses Subjects developed on a student's IEP to address various aspects of student need that are not specifically represented in the Ontario curriculum, in order for the student to learn new skills. These may include areas such as social skills, communication skills, or money management, depending on individual need. At the high school level, these would not be given formal credits.

American Sign Language (ASL) The primary visually perceived language in North America, it uses hand gestures, their placement relative to the body, as well as facial expressions and other body movements to communicate meaning.

Antecedent-Behaviour-Consequence (ABC) form (or chart) An assessment tool to examine the frequency and causes of certain undesirable behaviours. The form includes three columns to record the antecedent (what happened just before the behaviour, or the "trigger"), the undesirable behaviour that occurred, and the consequence.

Antecedent strategy Strategy used to prevent problematic behaviours by adapting the environment, informed by previous identification of antecedents that occur prior to the behaviour.

Applied-level course A course that develops student knowledge and skills through a focus on foundational concepts, practical and concrete application, and real-world examples. Applied-level courses lead to a future in college, an apprenticeship, or direct entry into the workforce.

Assessment summary The report provided by the clinician who completes an assessment. It contains a summary of the results of the assessment as well as suggestions for treatment/intervention.

Assistive technology Specialized software and/or hardware that adapt how specific tasks can be performed to meet the needs of the user.

Association for Community Living An organization that supports individuals with intellectual disabilities through community participation. The organization provides leadership and engagement programs, organizes awareness campaigns, and supports research in promoting equality.

Auditory learning A learning style in which an individual depends on hearing as a main method of comprehending and retaining incoming information.

Autism Spectrum Disorder (ASD) A complex neurobiological condition that is primarily evident by difficulties in social communication skills and restricted/repetitive behaviours. The use of "spectrum" refers to the continuum of severity, symptomology, and functioning that individuals with ASD exhibit.

Behaviour assessment Aimed at verifying the behavioural needs of an individual. A common tool used in Ontario to assess behaviour is "The Child Behaviour Checklist" by Achenbach and Edelbrock.

Behaviour Support Plan A written plan that targets the underlying purpose of undesired behaviour, replaces that behaviour with something more appropriate, and reduces or eliminates the undesired behaviour.

Belonging Feeling affinity for, and being welcomed and seen as, a member of a place or group.

Bi-modal Two modes of instruction or learning. For example, both lectures and a mentorship program on the same topic.

Blind and Low Vision Formal category of an exceptionality that falls in the category of "physical," as identified by an IPRC; a diagnosed medical condition involving the inability or reduced ability to see.

Break card A tool that provides a student with the option to ask for a break when feeling frustrated. A break card can be a very simple card with the word "break" on it or a picture of a quiet area. The student provides the teacher with the card when a break is needed. Alternatively, the teacher can provide the student with the break card if the need for a break is evident.

Broad-based benchmark In Ontario, broad-based benchmark assessment is conducted province-wide, testing students' literacy and math skills to assist school boards in determining areas for growth in student achievement, teacher professional development, and needed resources. The test results are available to teachers, parents, students, and the public. The assessment is carried out at key stages of student learning by the Education Quality & Accountability Office (EQAO).

Bullying Aggressive behaviour meant to cause harm, fear, or distress that is typically repeated over time. Bullying occurs in a situation where there is a real or perceived power imbalance.

Canadian Cognitive Achievement Test (CCAT) The CCAT is a standardized, norm-referenced group test that measures verbal, quantitative, and non-verbal cognitive abilities for students in kindergarten to grade 12.

Cardboard cubbies Created with a trifold cardboard divider, these privacy screens can be used as a study carrel placed on top of a desk.

Central auditory processing The part of the brain that allows for the key auditory functions such as sound

discrimination, pattern recognition, sound localization, and temporal masking.

Character education Teaching and nurturing the universally positive attributes that provide a standard for behaviour, including academic achievement, respect for diversity, community citizenship, and partnership.

Child and youth worker A support staff member that has been trained to work with children and youth who have social, emotional, or behavioural difficulties.

Child Disability Tax Credit A tax-free benefit of up to $2,730 per year ($227.50 per month), as of 2017, for families who care for a child under age 18 with a medically certified physical or mental disability that has lasted, or is expected to last, for a continuous period of at least 12 months.

Chronic pain Any pain lasting more than 12 weeks. It may start from an initial injury, or there may be an ongoing cause, such as an illness. Fatigue, decreased appetite, mood changes, and other health problems including those related to limited movements (such as reduced flexibility, strength, and stamina) often accompany chronic pain.

Cognitive (ability) The constructs that allow individuals to acquire and retain knowledge, such as memory, organization, learning, understanding, reasoning, and attention.

Collaboration A method where a group of individuals work together to achieve a common goal. Each member's opinion and ideas are viewed as valuable and equal to each other's in a way to formulate solutions to a problem or completion of a task.

Communication: Autism Identification used by the Ontario Ministry of Education to describe a severe learning disorder characterized by change in rate of educational development; ability to relate to the environment; mobility; perception, speech, and language; and lack of representational symbolic behaviour that precedes language. It is analogous to the clinical definition of ASD but uses the categories and subcategories of school-based special education. See **Autism Spectrum Disorder** (ASD).

Communication: Learning Disability One of the IPRC's subcategories, relating to a learning disability that involves difficulty with receptive language, language processing, expressive language, or mathematical conditions. These usually result in a discrepancy between assessed intelligence and academic achievement.

Co:Writer® Word-prediction software that allows for text-to-speech capability and enables its users to recognize and select whole words by looking and listening rather than struggling with extensive keyboarding and spelling.

Cystic fibrosis A multi-system disorder that produces a variety of symptoms including persistent cough with mucous, wheezing, and shortness of breath; frequent chest infections; bowel disturbances; and weight loss or failure to gain weight despite increased appetite. Occurs when a child inherits, from both parents, the recessive gene mutation responsible for cystic fibrosis.

Developmental Coordination Disorder A motor skills–based disorder in which a delay in the development of motor skills or coordination, rather than an identifiable medical or neurological explanation, results in a child being unable to perform common, everyday tasks.

Diagnostic and Statistical Manual, **Fifth Edition** (*DSM-5*) Contains a listing of diagnostic criteria for every psychiatric disorder recognized by the Canadian health-care system.

Down Syndrome A naturally occurring chromosomal arrangement in which additional genetic material attaches to chromosome 21 during early cell division. Characteristics vary greatly but include mild to severe physical and learning implications.

Educational assistant Support staff person who may work with students individually or in small groups to deliver activities that reinforce and advance their learning.

Elopement A common trait of individuals with Autism Spectrum Disorders where they leave or "run away from" a safe, familiar area to cope with stress of external stimuli.

English Language Learners (ELLs) Students who are learning the English language at the same time that they are learning the curriculum being taught to them in English.

Enrichment Improving or enhancing the quality or value of education by going into the curriculum topics in more depth, making connections between sections of the curriculum, or learning beyond the curriculum.

EpiPen A brand of auto-injector that contains epinephrine; used as a first-line treatment for severe allergic reactions that may be life threatening.

Evidence-based practices Teaching practices that are evaluated as effective based on data gathered over time demonstrating their effectiveness.

Exceptionalities A word used in education (typically analogous to disability) to broadly describe individuals based on their level of need in relation to the developmental and physical domains for their age. A person is identified as exceptional in specific areas or as an overall learner.

Executive functioning Higher-order thinking processes involved in coordinating and controlling other cognitive abilities and behaviours. They include both organizational and regulatory functions such as planning, self-control, working memory, decision making, and abstract thinking.

Fetal Alcohol Effects (FAE) A condition in which children exhibit one or more developmental and behavioural difficulties to varying degrees, such as hyperactivity, poor coordination, learning or language difficulties, or seizures, but not all the criteria for Fetal Alcohol Syndrome are met.

Fetal Alcohol Spectrum Disorder (FASD) An umbrella term describing the range of effects that can occur in an individual whose mother drank alcohol during pregnancy. These effects include physical, mental, behavioural, and/or learning disabilities with possible life-long implications.

1st percentile The lowest percentile score (i.e., lowest score relative to the student's peer group), indicating a great deal of difficulty in the task being performed. See **Percentile**.

Five-point scale A visual system that can help to organize the thought process of an individual when confronted with difficult moments, particularly those that require social understanding or emotional regulation.

Breaking a previously determined problem area into five visually illustrated parts can support students during communication breakdown, and help them make sense of the reactions and feelings of themselves or others.

Flipped classroom Teachers create instructive videos and interactive lessons for at-home learning and review. Students watch and complete the material at home, and then do activities, homework-style problems, or collaborative learning on the studied concept while in the classroom—"flipping" the common instructional approach.

Frequency Modulation (FM) system A method of transmitting sound from a transmitter (worn by the speaker or teacher) to the listener's (or student's) hearing aid or other receiver in order to amplify a particular sound for the listener.

Full-time special education classroom A separate, self-contained classroom for children with physical, academic, cognitive, or social–emotional difficulties that cannot be accommodated in a regular classroom. These classrooms are legally restricted in size by Regulation 298, section 31 of the Education Act in Ontario.

(The) Functional Analysis Screening Tool (FAST) A questionnaire on the relationship or correlation between problematic behaviours and any antecedent and consequent events.

Function (of behaviour) The reasons(s) why a student engages in a particular behaviour. The accepted functions of behaviour are attention, escape, tangible, and sensory—or a complex combination of these.

Gifted An exceptionality characterized by an unusually advanced degree of general intellectual ability that requires a greater breadth and depth of learning experiences to satisfy the student's educational potential. High scores on psychoeducational assessments are usually required for entrance into a program but the specific requirements vary by board.

Guidance counsellor A school staff member whose role is to support students in their personal, interpersonal, and career development needs.

Home-schooling A system in which students do not attend formal publically funded education; rather, they learn curriculum-based information at home from someone who may or may not be an Ontario Certified Teacher.

Hush bottle One term for a sensory bottle; a clear bottle filled with liquid and glitter and then sealed. It can be used to help calm a frustrated or upset student.

Identification The process of using gathered information—including work samples, assessment data, observations, and experiences—to categorize students based on their learning needs in order to provide more accurate and focused programming for students.

Identification, Placement, and Review Committee (IPRC) Composed of at least three persons, one of whom must be a principal or supervisory officer of the board, the IPRC must decide whether and under what categories students should be identified as exceptional, decide appropriate placement for the students, and review their decision annually. Regulations 181/98 drive this process.

Inclusive Through deliberately chosen language and action, ensuring that all students can participate fully and that nobody is excluded or singled out.

Inclusive classroom A classroom environment where differentiated learning opportunities are created, and all students, regardless of ability, can learn and be supported together.

Individual Education Plan (IEP) A working written plan and legal record describing the special education program and/or accommodations required by a student, given the student's identified strengths and needs that affect the student's ability to learn and demonstrate learning; also functions as an accountability tool.

Individual Education Plan (IEP) software Any program that is designed for developing IEPs in an online environment, which allows for access by multiple professionals. The software is designed specific to the policies, procedures, and needs of a specific jurisdiction, such as a school board.

Individual Education Plan (IEP) team A group of individuals involved in caring for and educating the student for whom the IEP is being developed, who work collaboratively to develop the student's IEP. The group will vary based on the needs of the individual student.

Individual Program Plan (IPP) An individualized goal-based resource developed with child-care staff, parents, and resource consultants for children in child care, designed to help meet both the family's and the child's needs. The IPP can include training for family members and staff, as well as assessments of the child.

Intellectual disabilities An identification of an exceptionality as defined by the Ontario Ministry of Education in which the student's intelligence and information-processing speed is above the diagnostic category of mild mental retardation but below the low average range of intelligence.

Intelligence The ability to acquire, understand, and apply knowledge and skills.

Interdisciplinary Addressing multiple content areas, or disciplines, in one unit or course. For example, in education, a teacher may incorporate an interdisciplinary unit in Language and Health whereby students would participate in learning activities that include both Language- and Health-curriculum expectations. For example, students may create posters (Language) regarding the health effects of smoking (Health).

Interest inventory A method of assessment used to guide both teachers and students in forming a list of activities, subjects, and topics that a student enjoys. Students are asked a series of questions designed to help better understand themselves, their desires, their priorities, and their future goals.

Keeping It Together (KIT) A binder with a built-in organizational system for children with exceptionalities and their caregivers, developed by the McMaster Children's Hospital's CanChild research centre.

Kinesthetic learning Learning through movement and position of, and sensory input from, the body. Use of physical involvement and movement as part of the learning environment can engage those with a kinesthetic learning style.

Kurzweil An educational program or application for computer or tablet that provides text-to-speech, audio notetaking, highlighting, and multi-language capabilities for students.

Leadership The ability to effectively manage, inspire, and direct a group of people.

Learning disability (LD) An umbrella term for a wide variety of issues resulting from neurodevelopmental disorders that affect the ability to acquire, retain, understand, organize, and/or use verbal and/or non-verbal information; may be associated with difficulties in social interaction; and are not the result of hearing/vision acuity, intellectual disabilities, socio-economic factors, cultural differences, language barriers, lack of effort, or educational opportunities. This is outlined in PPM 8.

Learning strategies Practical plans of action to support academic success by ensuring students can obtain and retain information independently. These strategies may include literacy or numeracy skills, personal management skills (e.g., time management), and interpersonal and social skill development.

Learning Strategies credit Courses in grades nine and 10 that focus on providing practical plans of action to support academic success by ensuring students can obtain and retain information independently.

Learning styles inventory A tool designed to determine what learning variation (auditory, visual, oral, or kinesthetic) is best for an individual student in terms of both preference and ability.

Medical (needs) Physiological assessments—including vision, hearing, physical, diagnosis, or neurological—that provide information that might be helpful in understanding a student's characteristic requirements in the classroom.

Mental health diversion An option for an offender who has committed a minor criminal offence, and who has a mental health concern, in which the individual is required to seek mental health support in place of typical criminal justice consequences.

Mild Intellectual Delay (MID) A learning disorder characterized by lower than normal intellectual development, with the ability to learn in a regular class with the aid of considerable curriculum modification and supportive services; potential for independent social adjustment and economic self-support.

Modified courses Subjects or courses with changes made to the age-appropriate grade-level expectations in order to meet a student's learning needs. These changes may involve using expectations developed for a different grade level and/or increasing or decreasing the number and/or complexity of the regular-grade-level curriculum expectations.

Motivation Assessment Scale (MAS) An assessment that measures the function of problem behaviours in individuals with developmental disabilities with the goal of finding appropriate replacement behaviours. The MAS was created by Vincent Mark Durand and Daniel Crimmins.

Motor integration Output of physical movement in response to input from another sensory source (e.g., visual, auditory).

Multiple A combination of two or more school-based identifications including learning and other disorders, impairments, or physical disabilities that exist together for one student.

Multiple intelligences inventory An assessment method designed to measure a student's strengths and weaknesses in different intelligence areas in order to provide information on learning styles and capacities.

Non-credit (course) Instruction on a set of skills that students may opt to take but that does not earn them a credit towards completion of their Ontario Secondary School Diploma.

Occupational therapist Regulated professional who works with children to help develop their gross and fine motor muscle development when support is required.

Ontario Secondary School Diploma (OSSD) Certification of high school completion in Ontario. The diploma indicates completion of 18 compulsory credits, 12 elective credits, provincial literacy requirement, and 40 hours of community involvement.

Ontario Secondary School Literacy Test (OSSLT) A province-wide test, which all students take at the same time near the end of the grade nine year, used to measure whether students are meeting the minimum standard for literacy at that grade level. Successful completion of the test is required to earn a diploma.

Ontario Software Acquisition Program Advisory Committee (OSAPAC) The provincial body that develops, licenses, and promotes digital resources for education.

Ontario Student Record (OSR) The record of a student's educational progress, maintained and transferred from institution to institution, following the student throughout his or her educational career in Ontario.

Operationalized To express or define something, usually the cause of a behaviour, in relation to a series of assessments or trials that determine or prove the cause of the behaviour.

Percentile A type of converted score that is expressed relative to a student's group in percentile points. It indicates the percentage of students tested who achieved scores equal to or lower than the specified score. A score in the 60th percentile means that 59 of 100 students in that same group scored lower than that child.

Perceptual reasoning The ability to interpret and learn from visual input; identify, analyze, and predict visual patterns; think about objects in three dimensions; and use visual information about objects and patterns to reason, extrapolate, and solve problems.

Power Cards Cards written from the perspective of a character of interest for a child, to help the child make sense of routines, language, unwritten social rules, and other social situations. The cards relate the desired behaviour to the behaviour of their character of interest, and are designed to be a reference that the student can refer to at any time. The idea was first created by Elisa Gagnon in 2001.

Processing speed A measure of the ability to automatically and fluently perform relatively easy mental calculations in a timely manner, without thinking them through.

Profiles (student) A planning and information-gathering tool used to outline a student's strengths, needs, and the methods of assessment and instruction best suited to the student's learning-style preferences and needs.

Provincial school School that provides province-wide programs and services for students who are deaf, are hard of hearing, are blind, have low vision, are deaf-blind, and/or have learning disabilities.

Psychoeducational assessment A measure of the academic and cognitive competencies of children; categories of assessments administered include memory, planning, organization, writing, mathematics, and reading. These assessments are used to guide instruction and involve gathering developmental, family, school, social/emotional, personality/temperament, and health histories, and are administered or supervised by a psychologist.

Raven Standard Progressive Matrices (Raven SPM) An assessment method designed to measure a student's ability to reason by analogy and form perceptual relations, without relying on knowledge of language or requiring any formal schooling.

Red flag An indication of when it may be necessary to seek advice or assistance, or to engage in intervention.

Referrals Information submitted, usually by the resource teacher, to obtain specialized services, equipment, assessments, or treatments for a specific student requiring additional support. Each school board in Ontario varies on how referrals are completed at the school level; however, all requests for additional services must go to the board office for approval.

Regular classroom Conventional classroom that all students not assigned to an alternative classroom or school attend, averaging 20–30 students with a variety of abilities and learning needs in each, and organized by grade.

Relaxation station Also known as a calming corner or quiet corner, a relaxation station is an area in the classroom designed to provide a space for all students to access when they need a short break, quiet time to think through something they are frustrated with, or to regroup. The relaxation station contains comfortable areas to sit and may include sensory-based activities designed to provide a calming effect, and is an inclusive way to provide students the opportunity to de-escalate within the classroom.

Renzulli's triad Three overlapping spheres, representing the key qualities of creativity, task commitment, and above average ability, which intersect at the point of giftedness where all three traits are represented.

Resistance A refusal to comply with or be affected by something. Can take the form of avoidance as well as active disagreement and opposition.

Resource teacher A resource teacher has additional qualifications in special education, according to the Ontario College of Teachers, and works in a school to provide special education support to teachers and students within that school. The resource teacher helps to develop programs for students with exceptionalities, helps teachers to create and implement IEPs, completes some educational assessments, and liaises with school board personnel and outside agencies on behalf of students.

Resource team A group of individuals working at the school-board level with various areas of expertise in special education. The team supports resource teachers and schools in matters that require intervention and support beyond what the school can currently provide for a student. Members may complete more formal assessments, support schools with specialized training, observe students with significant needs and assist in implementing strategies and supports, and liaise with outside agencies.

Respect Treating yourself, those around you, and the physical environment with high regard and value. Listening, displaying proper manners, and following the rules are all indications of respect.

Response to Intervention (RTI) A tiered educational approach designed to provide assessment and instruction to students. At tier one, the curriculum informs assessment and instruction. If difficulties are noted, at tier two, an educator provides differentiated instruction or an intervention. If difficulties persist, at tier three, additional resources are sought to support the student's learning with more intensive, individualized interventions.

Restorative justice An approach to dealing with conflicts, with a focus on repairing the harm done to individuals and the community rather than on punishing the offender. The overall goal is to develop strategies to move forward without the offender repeating the same offences.

Reverse inclusion Having students from other classrooms visit and participate in special education classrooms, with the goal of facilitating reciprocal friendships and fostering improved social skills.

Safety plan A crisis-response plan designating responsibilities to staff members who are trained to intervene with students experiencing crisis. It can also be a plan developed at the school level for a student who, because of their behaviour, may pose a risk to him/herself, other students, staff, or others.

Scatterplot A scatterplot is a type of plot, graph, or diagram used to display patterns of behaviour over time.

Scoliosis A condition that leads to an abnormal curvature of the spine either to the left or to the right, affecting the chest and the lower back.

Seizures A short disruption, lasting from several seconds to over five minutes, in brain activity that interferes with its function, impacting behaviour and/or sensory function, such as movement, posture, memory, consciousness, vision, or hearing.

Self-advocate (noun) Someone who seeks support or awareness for a particular cause that affects them personally, and who recommends a particular position or action on their own behalf; (verb) to speak up for one's own needs.

Service dog A dog trained to do work or perform tasks for the benefit of an individual with a physical, sensory, psychiatric, or mental disability. For individuals with ASD, service dogs perform repetitive, non-verbal actions that are understood by these individuals, and also provide a sense of comfort and safety.

Sign language A system of visually perceived language that uses hand gestures, their placement relative to the body, as well as facial expressions and other body movements to communicate meaning.

Sleep disorder Difficulty initiating or maintaining sleep, or consistent disturbances in sleep patterns, or excessive feelings of sleepiness.

SMART A guide to goal setting. The acronym stands for Specific (simple, straightforward; who, what, where, why, and how?), Measureable (how much/many, what will be the definition of "accomplished"?), Achievable (realistic, able to be accomplished in the time and with the resources available), Relevant (worthwhile, matching your overall goals, the right time), Time-limited (has an end date, has steps to take towards overall goal).

Social justice Equal distribution of wealth, opportunities, and privileges within a society, including participation in the construction of reality as well as living conditions and material forms of measurement.

Social skills A set of behaviours that can predict social outcomes (positive or negative) for children and youth. Examples include co-operation, listening, friendliness, and conflict resolution skills.

Sound field device A tool that uses speakers placed throughout the classroom to project a designated speaker's voice, useful for individuals with hearing loss, learning disabilities, attentional difficulties, or developmental delays.

Special Equipment Amount (SEA) funding References any funding for equipment to help accommodate students with special education needs. Students do not have to be formally identified as exceptional to qualify.

Speech-language pathologist Health professional with the specialized skills and training necessary to provide prevention, identification, evaluation, and treatment of communication and swallowing disorders.

Statement of Decision A written document developed as an outcome from an IPRC meeting. It includes whether (and under which categories) the IPRC has identified the student as exceptional, the placement decision, recommendations regarding programs or services, the reasons behind the decision, and strengths and needs used to build an IEP (if the student is exceptional).

Strengths-based approach Emphasizes one's abilities as opposed to any difficulties or deficits. This approach is grounded in the belief that all individuals have unique potential, and that their personal realities must be understood in order to be successfully inclusive.

Stress balls Small, malleable toys in the shape of a ball designed to fit in the hand and provide sensory relief by squeezing.

Teamwork The sharing of knowledge or skills, working towards a common goal, commitment, and mutual accountability within a group of two or more individuals.

Time-out Following the occurrence of a problem behaviour, a student is given a time-out from attention to that problem behaviour, such as the activity, space, or peers who reinforced the problem behaviour. The goal is to prevent future displays of the problem behaviour.

Traumatic brain injury Caused by an object or force impacting violently with the head, or piercing through the skull and damaging brain tissue, often as a result of an accident or assault. A wide variety of short- and long-term symptoms include pain, memory impairment, sleep disruption, confusion, fatigue, nausea, mood swings, sensory impairments, and disorientation.

Universal Design for Learning (UDL) An educational framework to improve and optimize learning based on research in the learning sciences, including cognitive neuroscience; can accommodate individual learning differences.

Verbal comprehension The ability to understand, analyze, interpret, and express oneself using written words.

Video modelling Recordings or animations of individuals performing a desired skill, including clear step-by-step instruction and cues. Often used to teach individuals with disabilities a variety of social, academic, or functional skills.

Wechsler Individual Achievement Test (WIAT-III) A standardized academic achievement test used to measure knowledge in the areas of reading, written language, mathematics, and oral language.

Wechsler Intelligence Scale for Children (WISC) (Currently in version V) A psychological instrument used to measure intelligence in children. Structured in 16 subsets covering a range of areas, the WISC can help to identify specific learning or intellectual disabilities and strengths.

Wide Range Assessment of Memory and Learning (WRAML-2) An assessment that helps to determine the student's working memory capacity. It evaluates both short- and long-term memory as well as cognition (i.e., the ability to learn new material).

Woodcock-Johnson IV Tests of Achievement One of three components in a normed battery of psychoeducational assessments with a focus on academic performance, especially in math and language. Its purpose is to determine individual strengths, needs, performance patterns, and learning problems in order to support future interventions.

WordQ Word-prediction software that supports literacy and writing through a variety of features. Word lists, text-to-speech, language dictionaries, thesaurus, and suggestions based on similar spelling and sounds allow the software to be adapted to suit individual needs.

WordQ + SpeakQ Word-prediction software with a SpeakQ plug-in, which allows for the software to provide speech-to-text, pronunciation, and reading feedback capabilities.

Working memory The part of short-term memory, and other processing mechanisms, used to plan and carry out behaviour, and to retain concepts and facts in the midst of action. It is used to stay focused on a task, and to recall information currently in use (for example, focusing on a game and keeping the rules in mind while playing, or focusing on, remembering, and executing the next step in a recipe in the midst of cooking).

Written Expression A complex task requiring the integration of cognitive, linguistic, and motor abilities. Learning disability with impairment in written expression involves the inability to write, primarily referring to handwriting, but also coherence, occurring due to an issue in the brain related to orthographic encoding, not visual or motor impairment.

Index